# Joseph Carter Corbin

# Joseph Carter Corbin

*Educator Extraordinaire and Founder of
the University of Arkansas at Pine Bluff*

Gladys Turner Finney

BUTLER
CENTER
BOOKS
LITTLE ROCK, ARKANSAS

**The Butler Center for Arkansas Studies**
Central Arkansas Library System
100 Rock Street
Little Rock, Arkansas 72201
www.butlercenter.org

First edition: April, 2017
ISBN 978-1-945624-02-5

Manager: Rod Lorenzen
Book design: H. K. Stewart
Book cover design: Paul Hooven
Copyeditor: Ali Welky

All photographs and images used in this book appear courtesy of the author unless otherwise noted. The cover photograph of Joseph Carter Corbin is courtesy of the University of Arkansas at Pine Bluff Museum and Cultural Center.

Cataloging-in-publication data is on file with the Library of Congress.

Printed in the United States of America
This book is printed on archival-quality paper that meets requirements of the American National Standard for Information Sciences, Permanence of Paper, Printed Library Materials, ANSI Z39.48-1984.

Butler Center Books, the publishing division of the Butler Center for Arkansas Studies, was made possible by the generosity of Dora Johnson Ragsdale and John G. Ragsdale Jr.

To **Lieutenant Colonel Solomon J. Jameson,**
*U.S. Army, Retired, whose gift of research inspired
the writing of this book—and to all who cherish
the history of the University of Arkansas at Pine Bluff*

# Contents

# Acknowledgements

Like is the case for all writers, I am indebted to so many for their assistance in the preparation of this book. Heading the list are the reference librarians and staff at libraries, special collections, and historical museums who generously and painstakingly responded to all my questions; secured interlibrary loans, documents, manuscripts, and newspapers; and wished me well in my undertaking.

Kathryn M. Harris
*Library Services Director, Abraham Lincoln Presidential Library*

Stephanie Sims
*University of Arkansas at Pine Bluff Museum and Cultural Center*

Kitti Jackson
*University of Arkansas at Pine Bluff Museum and Cultural Center*

Shawna Woodard
*Genealogy Department, Dayton Metro Library*

Gregory Estes
*Interlibrary Loan Services, Dayton Metro Library*

Betty Hollows
*Historian, Ohio University*

William Kimok
  *Ohio University Libraries, Special Collections*

Kimberly Tully
  *Miami (Ohio) University Library*

John D. Cunningham
  *Athens County Historical Society and Museum*

Jana Meyer
  *The Filson Historical Society, Louisville, Kentucky*

Jennifer Oberhausen
  *University of Louisville, Archives and Special Collections*

Kristy Alexander
  *Executive Director, Pine Bluff–Jefferson County Historical Museum*

Lesley Martin
  *Chicago History Museum*

Gwen Podeschi
  *Abraham Lincoln Presidential Library*

Minnesota Historical Society, St. Paul, Minnesota

Sean Benjamin
  *Tulane University Research Collection*

Kay Thomason
  *Ouachita-Calhoun Genealogical Society*

Cincinnati Historical Society Library

LaToya Devezin
  *African American Resource Center, New Orleans Public Library*

Oberlin College Library

Gina Armstrong
  *John Parker Research Library, National Underground Railroad Freedom Center*

Regina Agnew
   *East St. Louis Public Library*

Douglas Magee, Victoria L. Norman, Colleen Phillips, and
      Arielle Emberson
   *Public Library of Cincinnati and Hamilton County*


Special thanks to the following: Henri L. Linton, director, University of Arkansas at Pine Bluff Museum and Cultural Center; Geoffrey Stark, Special Collections, University of Arkansas, Fayetteville; and the staffs of the Arkansas State Archives/History Commission, the Public Library of Cincinnati, and the University of Arkansas Museum and Cultural Center who diligently and without delay responded to my numerous requests and inquiries.

On equal par are the friends who provided a listening ear, assisted with the research, helped proof the manuscript, and accompanied me on research trips:

Linda McDowell
   *Little Rock, Arkansas*

Elveria Brown Goolsby
   *Dayton, Ohio*

Lee Townsel
   *Dayton, Ohio*

Bennie McRae
   *African-American Military Historian, Dayton, Ohio*

Joyce Coleman
   *President, African-American Genealogy Group-Miami Valley, Ohio*

Carla Coleman
   *President, Black History Commission of Arkansas*

Dr. Robert E. Jones
  *Dayton, Ohio*

Mack Arthur Lakes
  *Dayton, Ohio*

Paul Ohunni
  *Huber Heights, Ohio*

Natalie Walters
  *Dayton, Ohio*

Jose Jones
  *Dayton, Ohio*

Robert Harris
  *Yellow Springs, Ohio*

Angela Griffin Jones
  *Dayton, Ohio*

Beverly J. Gray
  *Director, David Nickens Heritage Center, Chillicothe, Ohio*

Toumani Rozier
  *Kettering, Ohio*

To these fine people, my deepest appreciation.

**— Gladys Turner Finney**
Trotwood, Ohio
2017

# Preface

First and foremost this book celebrates the life and legacy of Joseph Carter Corbin and his twenty-seven years as principal of Branch Normal College, now the University of Arkansas at Pine Bluff (UAPB). Corbin, the first African American Superintendent of Public Education in Arkansas, founded Branch Normal College at Pine Bluff and became principal of the school after legislation was enacted in 1873. Since that time, the school has been well known in Arkansas and among its peers. The school's tenure of more than 140 years of operation has earned it the distinction of being Arkansas's oldest institution of higher education for African Americans. As its founder, Professor Joseph Carter Corbin is considered the father of higher education for African Americans in Arkansas.

Joseph Carter Corbin was born on March 26, 1833, in Chillicothe, Ohio. He was the son of ex-slaves, William and Susan Corbin, and educated at Ohio University in Athens, Ohio. At what is now UAPB, Professor Corbin struggled to educate students and maintain an adequate physical facility with limited finances and many external interferences. Despite the school's stormy history, he produced the first bachelor degree

13

graduates. UAPB continues to graduate students of high quality who contribute immeasurably to the quality of life and progress of this nation.

Professor Joseph Carter Corbin—a man of distinction, high intellect, and learning—lived a full and fruitful life. He deserves greater recognition and preservation of his legacy for current and future generations. This book is intended to add to the storehouse of knowledge about this great educator and to inspire a collective reverence and memory among those who are heir to his legacy of education.

## CHAPTER 1

# Joseph Carter Corbin: Early Life and Family

Joseph Carter Corbin was born in the free state of Ohio on March 26, 1833. Ohio gained statehood in 1803 and soon passed residence requirements in the Act of 1804 to "regulate black and mulatto persons" who entered the state. Black and mulatto people entering Ohio had to register with the county clerk and present a certificate of freedom. No white person could employ them without certification. The act of 1807 declared that no black or mulatto person could enter the state unless, within twenty days, two white men signed a five- hundred-dollar bond, guaranteeing his good behavior and independent support. These laws would become the prototype for black codes, restricting the rights of African Americans in Indiana, Illinois, and the Michigan Territory. Ohio would become bitterly divided over the issue of slavery, and many of its citizens became active in the abolitionist movement and the Underground Railroad. The religious denominations in Ohio engaged in the most oppositional stance against slavery were the Quakers, the Baptists, the Methodists, and the Presbyterians.

Joseph Carter Corbin, a free man of color, was born in Chillicothe in Ross County, Ohio, the son of former slaves, William Corbin and Susan Mordecai Carter Corbin. William Corbin was born about 1798 in Virginia. The circumstances of his freedom are unknown. Freedom at the time was gained by the act of running away, purchase, manumission, moving with one's slave owner to a free state, or birth in a free state. William Corbin's registration document with the Ross County, Ohio, Clerk of Court on January 20, 1825, does not show proof of freedom. Per the 1807 Registration Act, William Corbin, entered into a (surety) bond together with Walter Dunn and Abraham Nickens as said security for a sum of five hundred dollars.[1] This was to ensure William Corbin's good behavior and independent support, without public assistance. The "free colored" population of Ohio was 9,568 in 1830; 17,342 in 1840; and 25,279 by 1850.[2]

William Corbin was baptized at the First African Baptist Church of Christ of Chillicothe in 1824, the year of the church's founding. The pastor was the Reverend David Leroy Nickens, who was an ex-slave, an abolitionist, an Underground Railroad conductor, and the first African American to be ordained as a minister in Ohio. The church and its members were actively involved in assisting runaway slaves in escaping to freedom along the Underground Railroad.

Many of the members were skilled craftsmen and property owners in the community. The church later changed its name to First Anti-slavery Baptist Church of Chillicothe. In 1836 Rev. Nickens and his family moved to Cincinnati, where he became one of the founders of the African Union Baptist Church. The Minute Book shows that William Corbin was acting as church clerk at First Baptist in 1838, and in 1840 was part of a committee that examined the church books.[3]

Susan Mordecai Carter was born in Virginia in 1804. When she registered on July 1, 1822, with the Ross County Clerk of Court pursuant to the law "regulating blacks and mulatto persons," she was described as a "girl of light complexion five feet four and one quarter inches in height, about nineteen years of age with a scar in the palm of her right hand and a small scar on the right ear with holes in her ears and straight long brown [hair], emancipated by John Parkhill by deed #366 of emancipation recorded at the Henrico County Court House and identified by John Parkhill." In 1790, Henrico County, Virginia, had 5,819 slaves, one of the largest number of slave populations in Virginia; it also had one of the largest populations of free black inhabitants.[4]

Susan Carter joined the First African Baptist Church of Christ of Chillicothe in October 1824. She was received into membership by a letter from the First Baptist Church of Richmond, Virginia. The First Baptist Church of Richmond, where Susan Carter was affiliated prior to coming to Chillicothe, was organized in 1780. In that year, Richmond was a town of 1,800 inhabitants, half of them slaves.[5]

The First Baptist Church of Richmond was the first church of any denomination to be organized in Richmond; the first in America to send its own members as foreign missionaries to the continent of Africa; and the first in the world to organize within its own membership an African Baptist Missionary Society.[6] The membership of First Baptist Church was made up of whites and their slaves, and free blacks. Lott Cary and Colin Teague were affiliated with this church. Both were born slaves in Virginia but became pioneer African American Baptist missionaries to Africa. In 1827, there were ninety-two white male members of the church; there were 1,165 female and black members. The Richmond Baptists were opposed to hereditary slavery and supported colonization of free African Americans back to Africa as a "way of righting the wrongs done to them." According to a history of the church, "The second era in the life of the church closed with a membership of 936, all of whom were white....Richmond Baptist Church was true to its New Testament prototypes....As in the days of our Lord, 'the poor had the gospel preached unto them.' Negro slaves heard the gospel message as proclaimed by Pastor Courtney, accepted the Savior he presented...and were baptized."[7]

William Corbin and Susan Mordecai Carter were married on January 23, 1825, in Ross County, Ohio. They had a large family. Joseph was the oldest son. The following are the children traceable in the federal population census, with their estimated birth years: Margaret P. (1824); Susan (1829); Elizabeth (1830); Joseph (1833); Isabella (1833); William B. (1836); Lucy (1837); John (1841); Mary (1843); Henry (1845); and Margaret A. (1845).[8]

By 1850, the Corbin family had moved to Cincinnati, Hamilton County, the 8th Ward. Cincinnati had a free black population of 3,600 in 1850. There were opportunities for education for their younger children, as Cincinnati was the first settlement in the Northwest Territory to have a public school system. According to historian W. P. Dabney, "The Colored people of Cincinnati were progressive in their pursuit of education. By 1852 they had fully established and organized schools under their own board of six trustees, later increased to nine."[9] Cincinnati was a hotbed of abolitionist activity. In 1852, Harriet Beecher Stowe of Cincinnati published her famous novel *Uncle Tom's Cabin*.

Both William and Susan Corbin lived long lives. William worked as a porter in Cincinnati. In 1870, however, he was described in the federal population census for Ohio as seventy-two years old and "infirm." Susan's age was listed as sixty-nine. Susan Corbin preceded William Corbin in death, dying on February 9, 1874, at her residence: 141 Smith Street, Cincinnati. William died on January 29, 1875, in Cincinnati.

## CHAPTER 2

# Education:
# Life at Ohio University

Education and religion were highly valued by Joseph Carter Corbin and his family. Young Corbin received his primary education in the subscription schools of Chillicothe, and he was then schooled at home and in boarding situations. Private instruction was the only means of education prior to the establishment of common schools. The Act of 1825 established free common schools in Ohio but, according to educational historian James J. Burns, "no common school entirely free can be said to have existed until the School Law of 1838."[1]

Between 1848 and 1850, Corbin attended the boarding school of the Reverend Henry Adams, a prominent Baptist minister and educator in Louisville, Kentucky. There, he served in the dual role of student and teacher's assistant. Adams was proficient in languages and likely facilitated Corbin's preparation to enter Ohio University at an advanced level.

Founded a year after Ohio was admitted to the Union, Ohio University was established by an act of the legislature on

February 18, 1804. It was first called American University. The first three students were enrolled in 1808. According to Ohio History Central, by the late 1800s, Ohio University had taken a leading role in providing education and training to Ohio's future teachers. The goals of the university were to provide skilled teachers and to establish standards in public education.[2]

In the fall of 1850, when the vast majority of African Americans and "mulattos" were in slavery, seventeen-year-old Joseph Carter Corbin enrolled at Ohio University as a sophomore. That same year, the "separate but equal" doctrine was established in a school integration lawsuit in Boston. The Fugitive Slave Law of 1850 established a bounty on runaway slaves. When Corbin entered Ohio University, Alfred Ryors—a Presbyterian minister and mathematics professor—was the president (serving from 1848 to 1852). According to Betty Hollow's history of the school, there were rules of conduct against immoral behaviors and the possession or exhibition of lascivious, impious, or irreligious books or ballads. Also forbidden were lying, profanity, drunkenness, theft, uncleanliness, and unlawful games. Students were expected not to "quarrel, insult, and abuse a fellow student." They were to "treat all persons with modesty, civility and respect."[3]

To receive a degree, Corbin was required to be proficient in the works of Virgil, Horace, Cicero, Xenophon, and Homer; the Greek Testament; geography; logic; arithmetic; algebra; conic sections; natural philosophy; and the general principles of history, jurisprudence, English, grammar, rhetoric, belles letters, criticism, surveying, and navigation.

Literary societies were popular at the time, and Corbin belonged to the Ohio University Philomathan Society. Hollow stated, "With little to do except study, these young men formed literary societies…and spent hours honing their skills in debate, oratory, essay writing, reading, and interpretation of literature."[4]

There were no dormitories at Ohio University. However, there were some student accommodations on campus, at which Corbin most likely would not have been allowed to stay. He would have likely boarded in the community.

The "free colored" population in 1850 of Athens County, Ohio—where Ohio University was situated—was 106 out of a total population of 18,215. These 106 citizens lived in seven of the fourteen townships. Educational opportunities were available to them at the Albany Manual Labor Academy, opened to all races, until the academy was taken over around 1863 by the Disciples of Christ Christian Church, which refused further admission to the black community. The academy had attracted students from all over the United States, including a young Texan of color, Milton Holland, who won the Congressional Medal of Honor for his service in the Civil War. There was an active Underground Railroad in Athens County, and the owner of the newspaper called for the abolition of slavery.

In 1853, when Corbin graduated with a Bachelor of Arts degree, Solomon Howard was the president of Ohio University. Corbin had become the third African American student at Ohio University. The first African American student was John Newton Templeton, a freed slave. He received his diploma in 1828 and became an educator, a newspaper publisher with Martin Robinson Delaney, and an officer of the Pittsburgh Anti-Slavery Society. The second African American student was Edward J. Roye, who came to Ohio University in 1833 and later became the fifth president of the Republic of Liberia.[5]

Corbin came of age at an ominous and turbulent time in American history for African Americans. Enacted were the Missouri Compromise of 1850 and the Kansas-Nebraska Act of 1854, which repealed the Missouri Compromise and opened northern territory to slavery. The United States Supreme Court

(1857 *Dred Scott* decision) denied citizenship to African Americans and declared that blacks had no rights that whites were bound to respect. There was also the emerging Back-to-Africa Movement for free blacks. How these events affected Corbin is unknown, as we do not have journals or memoirs by him on these matters. But for an educated free man of color, these events had to be troublesome.

There is no evidence of overt racial hostilities against Corbin while he was at Ohio University. Corbin had significant advantages for the times. Born free into an intact family, without personal subjugation to the evils of slavery, he was able to obtain a superior classical education. He was also fair complexioned and could easily be perceived as white. In the 1850 census, he was described as mulatto; in the 1870 census, he was enumerated as white.

According to school records, Joseph Carter Corbin received two Master of Arts degrees from Ohio University, in 1856 and 1889, respectively. He completed the course work and examinations for the degrees, although there are differences of opinion whether a thesis was required at this time.[6]

## CHAPTER 3

# The *Colored Citizen* and Corbin during the Civil War

According to historian W. P. Dabney's 1926 *Cincinnati's Colored Citizen*, "Cincinnati, up to the outbreak of the rebellion, largely sympathized with the slave-holders....Many of the leading families by blood and kindred were connected with the South; indeed largely came from there. Through trade with the South its citizens had been greatly sustained. The establishment of an anti-slavery newspaper had resulted in its destruction by a mob, in which were some of the most prominent citizens.... The quarters of the Negro population were subject to attacks... aided by the rabble from the Kentucky Side of the Ohio. Free speech, if it took the form of public protests against the continuance of slavery, was dangerous."[1]

There is no evidence Corbin volunteered in one of the Ohio Volunteer Units of Colored Soldiers during the Civil War. Five thousand Ohio African American troops served in state or federal units. The 27th U.S. Colored Infantry Regiment, recruited by John Mercer Langston, with the authorization of Governor

David Todd, was organized into service on January 16, 1864, at Camp Delaware, Ohio.

During the Civil War, Corbin worked as a clerk for the Ohio Valley Bank and the Third National Bank of Cincinnati. He was engaged in the publication of a weekly newspaper, the *Colored Citizen* (1863–1869) with co-editors John P. Sampson, Charles W. Bell, H. F. Leonard, and the Reverend George Williams. According to the Ohio Historical Society's *African-American Experience in Ohio, 1850–1920*, "The *Colored Citizen* was established November 7, 1863…by an association of colored residents of Cincinnati, Louisville, Zanesville, St. Louis, Chicago, Columbus, Indianapolis, and other major cities in the Midwest. It was primarily a journal of general news and literature with an emphasis on news pertinent to African-Americans. The editors considered the press as the most powerful tool in refuting lies and slanders of critics of African-Americans."[2]

Examples of important issues and news items that appeared at this time in the *Colored Citizen* were "The Colored Public Schools of Cincinnati—Their Faults and the Remedies"; Frederick Douglass's stand against the plan of the Reconstruction Committee; the Convention of non-Episcopal Methodists meeting in Cincinnati; the adoption of a report "favoring the reconstruction plan of Congress"; and a committee of three "being appointed to investigate the Memphis Riots."[3]

Although Corbin did not serve, Corbin's brother, John H. Corbin, served in the Civil War from 1861 to 1865. John H. Corbin enlisted on October 16, 1861, at Camp Wood, Fond du Lac, Wisconsin. He fought as part of the 14th Wisconsin Volunteer Infantry, Company A. The 14th Wisconsin was mustered into federal service of the United States, January 30, 1862. He was promoted to Quartermaster Sergeant on August 31,

1862. He reenlisted on December 12, 1863, and was reappointed Quartermaster Sergeant. He was discharged on October 9, 1865, at Mobile, Alabama.[4]

## CHAPTER 4

# Marriage and Children

At the time of the 1860 census, Corbin's future wife, Mary Jane Ward, was a twenty-seven-year-old "Free Inhabitant" and a dressmaker. She lived in the East Half of the 15th Ward of Cincinnati. Her thirty-year-old sister, Eliza Gaines, lived in the 13th Ward.[1]

Corbin married Mary Jane Ward on September 16, 1866, in Cincinnati.[2] In 1870, Eliza Gaines was living in Cincinnati with the Corbins and their two young sons, John and William. Eliza followed the family to Arkansas and likely assisted Mrs. Corbin with caring for the Corbins' five children.

## Descendant Chart for Joseph Carter Corbin and Mary Jane Ward Corbin:

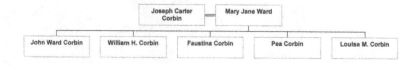

## John Ward Corbin

**Born:** 1867, Cincinnati, Ohio.

**Education:** Attended Preparatory School at Branch Normal College and Oberlin College. LI degree from Branch Normal College, Class of 1888.

**Occupation:** Dentist.

He died December 8, 1907, in Pine Bluff, Jefferson County, Arkansas, from meningitis. Reinterred December 27, 1909, Waldheim German Cemetery (now Forest Home), Forest Park, Illinois, from Oak Woods Cemetery in Chicago.[3]

## William H. Corbin

**Born:** 1869, Cincinnati, Ohio.

**Education:** Attended Preparatory School at Branch Normal College. He was "the graduate of a large eastern university" and considered "one of the smartest Negroes in Arkansas."

**Occupation:** Stenographer and teacher.

He died October 6, 1929, in Pine Bluff, Jefferson County, Arkansas, from a skull fracture due to a homicide, which was never resolved. Buried October 10, 1929, Waldheim German Cemetery (now Forest Home), Forest Park, Illinois.[4]

## Faustina Corbin

**Born:** Circa 1873, Little Rock, Arkansas.

She died August 1, 1884, in Little Rock, Arkansas, due to diphtheria. She was reinterred February 20, 1886, at Union Baptist Cemetery, Cincinnati, Ohio, from Oakland Cemetery, Little Rock.[5]

## Pea Corbin

**Born:** Circa 1875, Arkansas.

Presumed to have died as a child in Arkansas. Place of interment could not be found.[6]

**Louisa Maude Corbin**

**Born:** Circa 1876–1880, Arkansas.

**Education:** Attended Preparatory School at Branch Normal College. Graduated from a school in Ann Arbor, Michigan, according to one source, but this could not be verified.

**Occupation:** Industrial Arts Teacher-Sewing.

Taught sewing at Branch Normal College; served also as Dormitory Matron. Date of death and place of interment could not be found.[7]

## CHAPTER 5

# New Ventures:
# Corbin Moves to Arkansas

It is not fully known why thirty-nine-year-old Joseph Carter Corbin chose to migrate to Arkansas in 1871. Arkansas had been admitted to statehood in 1836, seceded with the Confederate states in 1861, and was readmitted to the Union in 1868.

Following the Civil War, Reconstruction in the South meant freedom for the newly freed slaves. The Emancipation Proclamation in 1863 freed African American slaves in the states of rebellion, and the Thirteenth Amendment to the U.S. Constitution emancipated the remaining slaves. The Fourteenth Amendment granted citizenship to the former slaves and their descendants.

There was a great need for teachers in Arkansas, and a great desire for education by former slaves who had been prohibited from learning to read and write. Black common schools and colleges were founded during this time. There were 111,115 slaves in Arkansas in 1860; of the 144 free African Americans in Arkansas in 1860, five were reported attending school.[1] There were five black teachers in the state in 1866. According to historian David Calkins, "Because Corbin had participated actively in the political arena created by the Colored School System in Cincinnati, he was well-prepared for his new venture. The opportunity to assume leadership and the satisfaction and status of holding public office were largely sought by ambitious Blacks, so long denied a political outlet for their talents."[2] Corbin ran for trustee for the Cincinnati Colored School Board in 1870 for the Western District, as reported in the June 23, 1870, *Cincinnati Enquirer*. Nine trustees were elected, three for each district (the Western District, the Eastern District, and the Walnut Hills District). The Western District comprised "the entire city which was west of the east line of Vine Street."[3] Corbin served an earlier term on the Cincinnati Colored School Board, from 1864 to 1865.[4]

Many northerners came south to assist in the reconstruction effort. They were called "carpetbaggers," a pejorative term used by southerners who were suspicious of their intent and motivation. It was also a time of opportunity for the well-educated Joseph Carter Corbin, who was an experienced journalist and teacher. Corbin worked as a reporter for the *Daily Republican*, which was the official newspaper for the Republicans, and he was assistant postmaster for the U.S. Post Office in Little Rock. When Corbin arrived in post–Civil War Little Rock, the racial mores would have prohibited social mingling among the races. He would have affiliated with his own African-American church, fraternal order, and social organizations. There were freedmen's schools in Little Rock, established in 1865 under the Freedmen's Bureau Act of March 3, 1865. When Corbin arrived in Pine Bluff in 1875, riverboat travel on the Arkansas River would have been a common sight.

According to the *Encyclopedia of Arkansas*, "Historian James Leslie has described Pine Bluff's entering its 'Golden Era' in the

1880s. Because of cotton production and river commerce, the city drew many industries and public institutions to the area. In 1890, it was the state's third-largest city. It soon had the W. B. Ragland, Samuel Franklin, and M. L. Bell Gas Works, a public school system, and the Buck, Smart & Company Bank. Around 1881, the town's first railroad, the Little Rock, Mississippi and Texas (later purchased by the St. Louis, Iron Mountain and Southern), connected the city with Little Rock (Pulaski County), and Major C. G. Newman founded the county's most successful newspaper, the *Pine Bluff Commercial*. The Cotton Belt Railroad established its lines and main engine maintenance shops in Pine Bluff in 1894, making it the county's largest industrial employer until the Pine Bluff Arsenal was built in 1942."[5]

Pine Bluff, located forty-five miles southeast of Little Rock on the Arkansas River, would eventually become a center for African American life and education due to Branch Normal College. During Corbin's time, Pine Bluff's African Americans were second only to those in Little Rock in the influence they held within the Republican Party. Pine Bluff would boast of having some of the most successful and wealthy African American businessmen in Arkansas.

## CHAPTER 6

# Branch Normal College and Joseph Carter Corbin

Higher education for African Americans in Arkansas began when Branch Normal College (now the University of Arkansas at Pine Bluff) in Jefferson County was organized as a branch of Arkansas Industrial University (now the University of Arkansas in Fayetteville), with Joseph Carter Corbin as founder.

During the Reconstruction period in Arkansas following the Civil War, J. C. Corbin was elected Arkansas Superintendent of Public Instruction. This was accomplished in the election of 1872, making Corbin the first African American to hold this position. Corbin, an educated man of color, ran on the general Republican ticket. His role as Superintendent of Public Instruction authorized him to serve as president of the Board of Trustees of Arkansas Industrial University. Corbin's background made him the right person for the time to establish Branch Normal College and to advance the cause of higher education for African Americans in Arkansas. He was also on the right side of political power.

Corbin's opponent in 1872 was the incumbent, Dr. Thomas Smith, a physician who had served in Arkansas during the Civil War and afterward settled in the state.[1] According to the School Law of 1868, the Superintendent of Public Instruction was "to be elected by the voters every four years, maintain an office at Little Rock, make annual reports to the governor and biennial reports to the general assembly, apportion the school funds to the several districts...and exercise general supervision over common school interests throughout the state."[2]

Corbin took office on January 4, 1873. He served as Superintendent of Public Instruction under the administration of Governor Elisha Baxter. As president of the Board of Trustees of Arkansas Industrial University, he helped lay the foundation for Branch Normal College, guide the development of Arkansas Industrial University, and sign the contract for construction of the main building of the university, known as Old Main.

At a board meeting in Little Rock on March 5, 1873, Professor M. W. Martin of Pine Bluff and Mrs. Alida Clark of Helena, who were white missionary teachers to the Freedmen of Arkansas, appeared and "set forth their claims and views in regard to additional Normal Schools for the training of Colored teachers." In the early years of the work of the Freedmen's Aid Society, teachers were scare. In 1866, there were only five African American teachers in Arkansas. The supply of teachers had to come from the North. A resolution by Trustee Bennett "that a committee of three be appointed for the purpose of devising some practical method whereby the legislature may be induced to make some suitable appropriation for the purpose of establishing a normal school [meaning teachers' college] for the education and fitting of persons as colored teachers" was unanimously adopted. President Corbin appointed the said committee of three, which was made up of two Supreme Court justices—

John Emory Bennett and Elhanan J. Searle—and State Senator John Middleton Clayton from Pine Bluff (brother to United States Senator Powell Clayton).[3]

Senator Clayton's bill (Act XCVII, Arkansas General Assembly) was approved on April 25, 1873. It authorized Arkansas Industrial University to establish Branch Normal College under the care and management of the Board of Trustees for the convenience and well-being of the poorer classes, in a suitable site southeast, or east or south, of the county of Pulaski. It would be governed by the same rules and regulations as the principal college.

Section 2 of the act stated that pupils would be admitted in like numbers, upon the same conditions, and with like qualifications and recommendations as the principal college; "and it shall be the duty of said board of trustees and they are hereby required to furnish said Branch College with professors and teachers and other necessary employees equal in numbers, attainments and other desirable qualifications to those furnished and employed in said principal Normal College; now organized as a department in said university; and they shall prescribe the same books, the same course of study, like training and proficiency, as may be directed, adopted and required in said principal college and they shall confer upon graduates thereof like honors, commendations and degrees as may be had or given in said principal Normal College."[4]

"Section 6: Be it further enacted, that for the purchase of a site, the erection of necessary buildings, improvement of grounds, the purchasing of furniture and the organization of said Branch College, and the payment of professors and teachers for two years commencing with the fall term…of 1873 the sum of… $25,000 is hereby appropriated out of any money in the treasury not otherwise appropriated."[5]

This was a time of bitter political factions in Arkansas politics. A crisis occurred, known as the "Brooks-Baxter War," over the hotly contested governor's election of 1872. Corbin's tenure as Superintendent of Public Instruction ended when the Democrats regained control of the state legislature and a new constitution was adopted. Corbin, according to historian William J. Simmons, "with the other Republican officers, was turned out of office." Governor Elisha Baxter had claimed victory and office in 1872 over his opponent, Joseph Brooks, who never accepted the results and initiated legal action to have Baxter removed. In 1874, a crisis erupted when Brooks along with armed men seized the capitol from Governor Baxter. Both factions organized military forces and appealed to President Ulysses S. Grant. The U.S. attorney general decided in favor of Governor Baxter, and President Grant recognized Governor Baxter as the legitimate governor of Arkansas. Simmons went on, "When the Reconstruction government was overthrown and Corbin was out of office as Superintendent of Public Instruction in 1874, he left the state to teach at Lincoln Institute in Jefferson City, Missouri. While vacationing at his home in Little Rock, he was sent for by Governor Augustus H. Garland, and was engaged to go to Pine Bluff and establish the Branch Normal College."[6]

The original board members of Arkansas Industrial University were out of office after the Brooks-Baxter War. The new board, of which the governor was ex-officio member and chair of the Branch Normal College Committee, hired its former president, Corbin, on August 18, 1875, to run the new college at a salary of $1,000 a year. Corbin recommended a downtown residential rental for $300 a year from Colonel M. L. Bell for the location of the college.[7]

Arkansas Industrial University was established in 1871 in Fayetteville, located in northwestern Arkansas. The mission of the school at Pine Bluff was to train black teachers, who would teach the masses of African Americans freed from slavery. Its site would be strategically located near the center of the state's African American population. Accordingly, Pine Bluff was selected as an acceptable site. Professor Corbin opened Branch Normal College on September 27, 1875, at Sevier and Lindsay streets (present-day 2nd Avenue and Oak Street). According to historian Thomas Rothrock, the "school was housed in a one story, ell-shaped frame house facing north on Lindsay Street and with porches along the entire front and across the back to the ell."[8] All that remains of that first location is an Arkansas History Commission/State Archives marker.

On September 2, 1875, the *Pine Bluff Republican* newspaper wrote, regarding the announcement of the opening of the Normal School, that "from the time of the legislation little had been carried out regarding the design of the school owing to the intervening financial and political disturbances." A special committee of the Arkansas Industrial University Board, "consisting of Governor Augustus Garland, D. E. Jones, and Professor Wood E. Thompson, was appointed for the purpose of founding the branch in the city of Pine Bluff."

The news release, likely prepared by Professor Corbin, outlined the following:

> Tuition in the school will be free, the beneficiary is, however, required to enter into a written obligation to teach for two years in the schools of the state in consideration of three years' tuition. This regulation applies also to such beneficiaries of the preparatory department as will be able, after one year's tuition, to enter the normal school. The school will be opened upon rather a small scale at first but additions to the number of teachers, etc. will be made from time to time, as the necessities of the case may deem. As the school is supported by the state, it is of course, open to citizens generally,

and we hope to see a large number of our colored youth avail themselves of its advantages.[9]

For Professor Corbin to open Branch Normal College was a challenge beyond measure. The fledgling Branch Normal College had no students of college level in 1875–76, contrary to the admission standards of Act 97. He had to adjust the admission requirements to the level of the students and prepare them for college-level work. Contrary to the statutory requirements that Branch Normal College be furnished teachers, professors, and other staff the same as Arkansas Industrial University, Professor Corbin was the administrator and only teacher from 1875 to 1882. Rothrock stated, "Corbin at first not only taught all the subjects in a demanding academic schedule, but fell heir to the additional burden of the 'custody of the building.'…Asking for custodial help in 1884, his request was ignored by the board."[10]

Professor Corbin's first challenge was that of grading the school, standardizing the skills of students taught by various teachers, and introducing the proper textbooks. "Struggling to organize his school, Corbin began by classifying his students generally according to their reading ability. This done, he labored patiently to equalize their 'unequal attainments,' by teaching, first of all, good reading, good writing, and good drawing; to do, secondly, what he could to strengthen and equalize their arithmetic; and to introduce them, thirdly, to the elements of vocal music." Corbin used the grading method common at that time in education in Arkansas and throughout the nation, and not the grading system of today. In the average ten-grade school system of the time, the First Grade was the senior year of high school. Second Grade was the junior year. The Third Grade was the sophomore year. A student who advanced to the Fourth Reader was ready for the final two years of high school or prep school. Latin, algebra, geometry, trigonometry, history,

English, grammar, and composition were required to pass the college entrance examination.[11]

Another dilemma faced by Professor Corbin was what to do about students below the age requirement seeking admission to the college. During the second year, 1876–77, Professor Corbin rejected a large number of underage applicants. The only underage students remaining on the roster were those in attendance at the close of the previous school year. He had retained them because he did not wish them to lose the benefit of their prior training. He seemed optimistic that the underage applicants would, in a short time, cease to be a problem, as the Public School District of Pine Bluff had been in operation for eight months during the year, had three teachers (Mr. M. W. Martin, Mrs. Alice V. Jennifer, and Miss Betty Newly), and admitted students from any part of the state.

Collection of matriculation fees was another issue Professor Corbin faced. The university required that a $5.00 matriculation fee be collected from every student. Paid only once, it entitled a student to matriculate for four years. It was required of beneficiary students and tuition-paying students.

Professor Corbin's Second Annual Report (1876–1877) to the Arkansas Industrial University Board of Trustees outlined the condition of the school, difficulties overcome, and progress made. He reported that grading of the school had been carried out by dividing the school into three distinct grades, First, Second, and Third Grade, largely based on reading.

Irregular attendance, sickness, bad weather, "want of means,"—and even the death of an excellent student—had caused legitimate absences. The excellent student, Alexander Franklin, died from pneumonia caused by lack of suitable lodgings. One of the best students, Rufus Daugherty, became ill from pneumonia, which compelled him to return home to Calhoun County.

Besides academic exercises, there were general exercises that included vocal music, drawing, and a daily opening exercise of a Sabbath school lesson. Students were also encouraged to consult works of reference and Professor Corbin's personal library. All the students had shown progress.[12]

## Professor Corbin's 1875–76 Recommendations to the Board of Trustees:

1. Increase the attractiveness of the school as soon as possible. Submit a well-digested plan to the next legislature for necessary appropriations. Secure a more suitable building.

2. Secure an amendment of the law to remove the College to Little Rock where public schools were superior to Pine Bluff.

3. Make provision for an increase in the number of teachers. "The necessity of this, in order that the school may accomplish its purpose is so apparent as to need no argument."

4. Change to adapt the school to the necessities of its class of students: Regulate the matriculation fee over the entire period of the four years.

5. Provide by law a proper certificate from the Normal Department, equivalent to an examiner's license that would entitle holder to teach in the public schools of the state.

6. Publication and distribution of a circular and catalogue relating specifically to the Normal College Branch. "I have prepared such a circular and would particularly request the publication of not less than five hundred copies for distribution."[13]

June 15, 1877. The Branch Normal College Committee Response to Professor Corbin's Recommendations:

**1st** We deem it impracticable with the funds at the command of the Board to secure for the Branch Normal School a more suitable building at present.

**2nd** We recommend that Branch Normal School be not moved to Little Rock.

**3rd** When the number of students of the required age and possessing the requisite qualifications has reached forty we would recommend the employment of an assistant.

**4th** We think it inexpedient to make any change in the matriculation fee, as it would offer a premium to students to enter for short terms, and the fee, as cheap tuition, for a single term.

**5th** We think that the products of our Normal Schools should not be exempted from the requirement to procure Certificates from County Superintendents or Examiners.

**6th** We concur in a recommendation for a separate Circular should be issued representing the interests of the Branch Normal School, provided the amount of matter printed be limited to the giving such information as is absolutely needed by the Patrons of the school.[14]

"Beneficiaries" were students who received free tuition because they were unable to pay. The university's guidelines permitted 237 beneficiaries, certified by their respective County Judge, to attend the Collegiate Department and another 237 to attend the Normal Department. Because the black population was concentrated in the southeastern counties, however, Professor Corbin did not comply with the county-quota list used at the Fayetteville campus. In setting admission standards, Corbin followed the rule that any applicant who could read the Fourth Reader and had "some acquaintance with the fundamental rules in arithmetic and a corresponding standing in Penmanship and Geography" should be allowed to matriculate. Since Branch Normal had been founded for the "poorer classes," he treated nearly all his students as "normal beneficiaries," and collected very little in tuition and matriculation fees.[15]

Professor Corbin worked diligently to mold the school into a classical model, including courses in Latin and Greek. He was committed to a classical education and was convinced that black youth must build their future on something other than farming and its related work. Regarding the university's rules on age, admission standards, and quota system, Professor Corbin was not faulty in his reasoning that the university's regulations were written for white students, and "to adhere was impossible without imperiling the very existence of the school." He showed great courage to resist. But he was caught between adherence to the letter of the law versus the spirit of the law.[16]

Over the years, Professor Corbin faced other challenges and obstacles. When the dormitory he proposed was built, "the Branch Normal Committee was much perplexed about finding suitable persons to take charge of it." Professor Corbin "agreed to take charge of the management by moving his wife from Little Rock, receiving no compensation for either himself or his wife, and assuming the entire responsibility for fuel, light and provisions, charging $8.00 per month." The Branch Normal Committee "regarded the dormitory as somewhat of an experiment. They were unwilling to spend much money in its outfit."[17] By placing in the dormitory one thousand dollars of his personal furniture, Professor Corbin "managed to keep up appearances, so that the establishment would not be a discredit of the state." There were also problems with the flooding of the grounds. He constructed shallow drains, which were of great service but in very rainy weather were entirely inadequate. Despite the obstacles, Professor Corbin remained committed to the cause of educating his students.

## Original Seven Students

Robert Allen...............age 15, Monticello, Drew County
Samuel Wargraves......age 14, Monticello, Drew County
Angeline Vester..........age 13, Monticello, Drew County
Jessie Devine ..............age 12, Monticello, Drew County
Lucinda Alexander.....age 13, Pine Bluff, Jefferson County
John Neely..................age 9, Pine Bluff, Jefferson County
Jeannie Neely .............age 12, Pine Bluff, Jefferson County

Source: "Student Enrollment Roster, September 27, 1875." Corbin's Narrative Report 1875-1876, Branch Normal College Records (MC-1921, Box 1, Folder 10, Special Collections, University of Arkansas Libraries, Fayetteville).

## Branch Normal College and the Morrill Acts

The Morrill Land-Grant Act of 1862 allowed for the creation of land-grant colleges in each state that would teach agriculture, mechanical arts, and military tactics without excluding scientific and classical studies. Arkansas Industrial University, founded in 1871, was an original 1862 land-grant institution. To secure funding for the college, Professor Corbin proposed in 1889 that the University Board of Trustees include his campus in the land-grant mission of the university and described the type of facilities needed for training students in the mechanical arts.[18] The Morrill Act paid for all the teachers' salaries at Branch Normal College. The Arkansas Legislature provided maintenance funds out of the state treasury beginning in 1887.

However, a growing spirit of racism among members of the white community caused Corbin to reevaluate his position, and he reluctantly concluded that the school must broaden its base of support if it were to survive in a political atmosphere increasingly charged with racial tension.[19]

Corbin pressed for establishment of "industrial departments" for both boys and girls, and he eventually secured them. A carpentry and machine shop was established for boys, and instruction in sewing and cooking for girls was emphasized. Nevertheless, the greater number of graduates became teachers in the state's African American schools.[20]

The second Morrill Act (1890), aimed at the former Confederate states, required each state to show that race was not an admission criterion, or to designate a separate land-grant institution for persons of color. Those schools designated in the 1890 legislation became known as the historically black college land-grant institutions.[21]

According to historian C. Fred Williams, "Passage of the 1890 Morrill Act came at an opportune time for the struggling institution. Corbin saw that he could use the agriculture training aspects for colored youths that would be less threatening to the white community. Consequently, he turned his attention to qualifying the institution for these funds. According to the enabling legislation, the Federal government would fund the program but allocation of the funds would be decided by the states. Corbin and his colleagues spent weeks lobbying members of the Twenty-

Eighth General Assembly and their efforts were rewarded when Arkansas officially approved the act on April 9, 1891."[22]

## Early Teachers
## Branch Normal College
## 1875-1902

| | |
|---|---|
| Joseph Carter Corbin, Chairman, A.M. | *Physics* |
| James C. Smith, A.B. | *Mathematics—First Assistant* |
| Alice A. Sizemore, A.B. | *Language* |
| William Stephen Harris | *Superintendent of Shops* |
| A. E. Smith | *Assistant Superintendent of Shops* |
| Thomas G. Childress | *Second Assistant* |
| Annie C. Freeman | *Third Assistant* |
| Louisa M. Corbin | *Fourth Assistant—Sewing Teacher* |
| E. K. Braley | *Instructor—Machine and Blacksmith Shops* |
| C. E. Houghton | *Superintendent of Mechanical Arts Department* |

## Assistant Student Teachers

| | |
|---|---|
| N. J. C. Johnson | *Geography* |
| Stephen W. Crump | *Grammar* |
| Jacob W. Ricks | *History* |

Sources: Catalogue and Circular of Branch Normal College, Arkansas Industrial University, Pine Bluff, Year ending June 5, 1886; Catalogue and Circular of Branch Normal College, Arkansas Industrial University, Year ending June 8, 1800-1901; Arkansas Industrial Board of Trustees Minutes, June 13, 1899.

## Collegiate Graduates
## Branch Normal College
## 1882-1892

**1882:** James Carter Smith, A.B.

**1883:** Alice A. Childress, A.B.

**1884:** John Gray Lucas, A.B.
Alexander L. Burnett, A.B.
Celis W. George, A.B.
John P. Williams, A.B.

**1885:** John C. Calhoun, A.B.
Archibald B. Crump, A.B.

**1899:** Thomas G. Childress, A.B.

**1892:** John H. Harrison, A.B.

## Licentiate of Instruction (LI) Degree

The low number of bachelor's degrees awarded was due to the offering of the Licentiate of Instruction (LI) degree in 1886, which allowed students to teach after two years of instruction. According to Izola Preston and Marian Morgan's article, "Joseph Carter Corbin and the Normal School Movement," "This caused a drying up of the pool of candidates seeking bachelor degrees and caused the school to operate essentially as a junior college."[23] However, it is remarkable that these bachelor's degrees were awarded considering the times and circumstances, and that Branch Normal College actually started with elementary-level students. The Licentiate of Instruction degree would have been attractive to the vast majority of students with limited resources to pay for their education and aspiring to work as teachers without spending four years to earn a bachelor's degree. It is unlikely that Branch Normal College possessed the teaching resources to produce a large number of Bachelor of Arts degrees. The LI degree allowed the emerging public school system to thrive, a major contribution to secondary education in Arkansas with an available supply of African American teachers. This was the original mission of Branch Normal College: to train African American teachers for the public schools. It succeeded.

## Branch Normal Students

The first two students to receive the Licentiate of Instruction degree (class of 1886) were Jacob W. Ricks, who became a principal at Fordyce, and George W. Bunn of Bonham, Texas, who became a medical doctor.[24] Professor Corbin's son, John Ward Corbin, received the LI degree in the class of 1888 and became a dentist in Chicago.

One of the most accomplished students of Professor Corbin and distinguished graduates of Branch Normal College was John Gray Lucas, a native of Marshall, Texas, who grew up in Pine Bluff and received a bachelor's degree in 1884. Besides Corbin, he was the only other African American in Arkansas to hold a cabinet-level position in the state government during Reconstruction. A man of superior talents and abilities, Lucas was an honor graduate of the Boston University School of Law, the only black student in his class of fifty-two. He returned to Arkansas and was admitted to the state bar. Soon afterward, he was named Assistant Prosecuting Attorney for Pine Bluff and Jefferson County. He was appointed Commissioner for the U.S. Circuit Court, Eastern District of Arkansas. In 1890, he was elected state representative from Jefferson County. He later moved to Chicago, where he established a lucrative practice and gained a reputation as an expert in criminal law. In 1934, he was appointed Assistant U.S. Attorney in Cook County; he served until his death in 1944.[25]

The conduct of the students at Branch Normal was exemplary. Professor Corbin reported in his May 1893 Narrative Report to the Board that "during the existence of the institution, the Board of Trustees had in not a single instance, been annoyed by any outbreaks or disorder upon their part." The same was true of their standing in the community.[26]

Regarding "the fear that some of the students may have voted illegally in the Clifton R. Breckinridge–John M. Clayton Contest for Congress," Professor Corbin refuted the charge stating that "the Chairman of the County Committee failed to find a single instance of illegal voting when information he provided about the male students was compared with the Poll-books and tally sheets."[27]

CHAPTER 7:

# Successes of Professor Corbin
# and Branch Normal College

As early as 1875, Professor Corbin had recommended the construction of a new school building for Branch Normal College. A two-story brick building with classrooms and an assembly hall was erected on a twenty-acre site on the western edge of the city of Pine Bluff. In 1882, Professor Corbin and his students moved into the new facility. According to Corbin, "This was a wild tract of land, in almost the same condition as when Columbus discovered America, with only one house within a distance of a quarter of a mile. With my own hands, I cleared away the forest, burned the brush and chopped the trees for fuel for the school, thus relieving the state of considerable expense. The grounds by 1893 were valued by competent judges to be about $25,000, and were surrounded by a large settlement of respectable people."[1]

A dormitory for girls was built in 1887 which was under the supervision of Professor Corbin and Mrs. Corbin. Professor Corbin had recommended a dormitory for girls in 1882. The dormitory was a brick structure that housed thirty to forty students. Girls living in the dormitory were required to keep their own rooms and the halls clean and to assist in keeping the dining room and kitchen clean. They were not to visit one another's rooms except by invitation. Students boarding elsewhere were under the supervision of Professor Corbin and were allowed to board only in places approved by him.

The shop building for the Mechanical Arts Department was completed in February 1892. It was a brick structure housing a wood shop, blacksmith shop, machine shop, tool room, and boiler room.

By May 1893, ten classes had graduated from Branch Normal College. Among the graduates were three of Professor Corbin's teaching assistants and five of the six teachers of the public schools of Pine Bluff.[2] Corbin said, "A number of my graduates have pursued professional courses at such institutions as the University of Michigan, Boston University and the institutions of Nashville, Tennessee. A large number of these are now practicing medicine, pharmacy, teaching, and the ministry, and are in almost every instance, reflecting credit upon the institution in which they were trained, by their morality, intelligence, and correct deportment."[3] It was also reported that several of the girls had become so proficient in typing that they were working for various lawyers in the city.

In 1894, the enrollment at Branch Normal College reached 242. The growth of the school required a larger building, and the legislature of 1901 authorized $5,000 for an annex to the main building and $800 for enlargement of the shop building.[4]

A sewing department was established in 1897 with Professor Corbin's daughter, Louisa M. Corbin, as the teacher. Louisa M. Corbin had completed her training at Ann Arbor, Michigan. After one year of operation, the sewing department was considered an "unqualified success" with a recommendation by Professor Corbin to the Board of Trustees that Louisa's salary be increased to that of the other female teachers. Within a short time, many of the female students were able to make nearly all of their clothing.[5] Exhibits of art needlework won awards at the State Fair.

Other successes were the introduction of vocal music into the curriculum; equipping and cataloging the library, which housed more than 3,500 volumes; and submission of a student exhibit for the Jefferson County Display and Chicago Exposition. The exhibit included several hundred emancipation papers and students' work. Branch Normal's exhibit compared favorably with those of other institutions, according to Professor Corbin, and the institution gained an award (Number 13,331) from the Chicago Exposition for literary work.

## CHAPTER 8

# Joseph Carter Corbin
# and Booker T. Washington

According to the *Pine Bluff Graphic*, "Professor Corbin was an educator who was well known throughout the state and the south on account of the important positions he held during his career. He was regarded as one of the most learned of his race, and had even been compared with Booker T. Washington by his intimate friends. He was distinguished by official positions in the postal service in this state and high position as an educator of Negroes. The most brilliant accomplishment...was his establishment of, and presiding over, the Branch Normal College in this city for thirty-years."[1]

The comparison to Booker T. Washington is intriguing. Other than the fact that each man is a founder of a school of higher education for African Americans (an elite group in itself), the two men are opposites by circumstances of birth, education, and educational philosophy. And unlike the scholarship on Booker T. Washington, there is little published material on Corbin. There is also no evidence that Professor Corbin entered into the national debate with Professor Washington and Dr. W. E. B. Du Bois over the education of African Americans. It is unlikely too that Professor Corbin would have been southern whites' idea of a poster boy for liberal arts education for African Americans.

Booker T. Washington was born a slave on a Virginia plantation in 1856. He was a son of the slave master. He had no surname and chose Washington, after President George Washington, following emancipation. He was educated at Hampton Institute in industrial education. He opened the Tuskegee Institute in 1881 with a $2,000 appropriation from the Alabama legislature.

In contrast, Joseph Carter Corbin was born free in Ohio in 1833, although his parents had been former slaves in Virginia. He was not subjected to the personal evils of slavery. He had a surname, came from an intact family, and was the recipient of a classical liberal arts education at Ohio University.

After Frederick Douglass's death, Booker T. Washington, according to historian John W. Cromwell, "forged to the front as the foremost American Negro in the new dispensation of freedom through industrial opportunity and became the one man in the eye of the American public regarded as the leader of his race."[2] Almost every African American child has heard of Professor Booker T. Washington and his Tuskegee Institute through books, from commemorative coins and stamps, and during Black History Month.

Professor Booker T. Washington's approach to education and principles of industrial education grew out of his observations and experiences of the condition of his people. He believed that it was in the best interest of the mass of African Americans, who were impoverished and illiterate post slavery and Reconstruction, to be educated in the crafts and industrial skills. Tuskegee Normal and Industrial Institute was incorporated by the state of

Alabama as a normal college to train teachers. Professor Washington wanted to give his students such an education "as to fit a large proportion of them to be teachers, and at the same time cause them to return to the plantation district and show the people there how to put new energy and new ideas into farming as well as into the intellectual and moral and religious life."[3] He wanted his students who were moving from the farms to the cities to have marketable skills.

The Tuskegee Institute would become well known for its agricultural experiments. Students were given a practical education in life skills, "things everyone needs to know and think about and things that concern the welfare of their local community,"[4] according to Washington's *Up from Slavery*. The curricula included household economics, domestic work, nursing, agriculture, trades with academic work, blacksmithing, bricklaying, plastering, carpentry, cabinet making, machine work, painting, shoe making, steam fitting, plumbing, tinsmithing, tailoring, upholstery, and wheelwrighting. Bible study was an important part of the curricula.

In contrast to Booker T. Washington, Professor Corbin's approach to education was steeped in the classical tradition of education, and he embraced the study of the liberal arts and sciences as opposed to vocational study. The emphasis was on developing the mind or intellect, to think and reason analytically, and to have self-expression through languages and the arts. Professor Corbin's mission was to "train teachers for the common schools of the state."[5] His curricula in his preparatory department laid the foundation for the classical course of study for the Bachelor of Arts degree and the Licentiate of Instruction degree.

Professor Corbin's classical education at Ohio University made it possible for him to teach all primary and secondary classes and the higher-level courses in the collegiate department at Branch Normal College. With Corbin's request and designation of Branch Normal College as a land-grant institution, he expanded the curricula to include mechanical arts for male students and home economics and typing for female students.

What is extraordinary about Professor Corbin is that he began to successfully educate teachers at Branch Normal College for the emerging common schools of Arkansas only a decade following the Civil War. When Professor Corbin was the academic head of both the collegiate department and the normal school, his exemplary leadership in education extended to establishing teacher training institutes, co-founding the first black state teachers' organization, and serving as its first president.

## CHAPTER 9

# Controversy Concerning Corbin's Demotion

Booker T. Washington's plan for industrial education to teach black students mechanical rather than academic skills caught on and spread around the country, attracting the attention of Board of Trustees member William Henry Langford, a wealthy white Pine Bluff businessman and president of Citizens' Bank. He was appointed to the university's board in 1889, rose to become "Agent of the Board" for Branch Normal College, and later became chairman of the board. Agent of the Board was a powerful position that allowed Langford to run Branch Normal College. He served on the board until 1907. The duties of the Agent of the Board were not specified in the board's minutes, but the minutes showed that Trustee Langford was involved in insuring the mechanical shops, guaranteeing the treasurer surety performance bond, and approving and authorizing expenditures.

Langford held great interest in the development and operations of Branch Normal College and was instrumental in 1891 in securing state funds for building and equipping the industrial shops. In 1892, Langford hired William Stephen Harris, a white man and graduate of Miller Manual Training School in Virginia, to take charge of the shops. He also hired an assistant, A. E. Smith.[1] Trustee Langford was "ambitious to convert Branch Normal College into an Arkansas Tuskegee,"[2] modeled after Booker T. Washington's program. In doing so, however, he would usurp Professor Corbin's authority over the school with concurrence of the board and the complicity of Professor Harris.

Professor Corbin's success as an educator did not protect him from harassment by the state legislature. After a joint Senate-House Legislative Committee investigation "by Corbin's white Jefferson County enemies" of Branch Normal College in April 1893, which seemed politically motivated, and a recommendation that he be fired for alleged financial and managerial inability, he was relieved of his administrative responsibilities. Professor Harris, the white superintendent of shops, was made treasurer of Branch Normal College, with the responsibility for student admission, fee collection, and reporting to the Board of Directors. Trustee Langford ran the school and Professor Harris was his "right-hand man" on campus.[3]

Professor Corbin was charged with violating the admissions quota, admitting poor students without payment, and neglecting the normal features of the school. According to Rothrock, "The trustees at their June meeting in 1893 did not fire the sixty-year-old Corbin; neither did they have the courage nor the decency to defend him. They compromised by keeping him on as principal, but humiliated him by robbing him of nearly all power over the school and the students.... It was an act in keeping with the rising Age of Jim Crow in Arkansas, to place this white 'treasurer' in charge of the Negro School, but it was nonetheless as ruthless a piece of ingratitude and as cowardly a compromise as the trustees ever perpetrated."[4]

# Photograph Album

*Joseph Carter Corbin, Ohio University Alumni Bulletin, April 1909. Courtesy of University of Arkansas Libraries, Special Collections, Fayetteville.*

*Louisa M. Corbin.*

*Joseph C. Corbin (center) and Branch Normal College musicians are pictured in this ca. 1889 photograph.*

*Joseph C. Corbin and his students pose for a photograph on the south porch of the main building in 1892. Effie Stewart Wiley (mother of Frank Wiley) is seated at the left end, second row.*

*Branch Normal College, ca. 1882.*

# BRANCH NORMAL/AM&N

Branch Normal School was created April 25, 1873, as a branch of what is now the U. of A. Instruction began in 1875 in a house at Sevier and Lindsay Streets (2nd & Oak)- seven students enrolled. In 1882 the school was located west of Pine Bluff. The institution became Agricultural, Mechanical and Normal College in 1932. In 1972 AM&N was merged with the U. of A. and designated the University of Arkansas at Pine Bluff. This merger re-joined the two oldest public higher educational institutions in the state.

DONATED BY: GRADUATE & UNDERGRADUATE GREEK ORGANIZATIONS

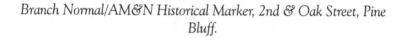

*Branch Normal/AM&N Historical Marker, 2nd & Oak Street, Pine Bluff.*

*J. C. Corbin Training School, AM&N College, ca. 1953. Courtesy of the University of Arkansas, Pine Bluff, Museum & Cultural Center.*

*J. C. Corbin High School, ca. 1950.*

*Aerial View, UAPB, ca. 1940s.*

*Early Branch Normal College choir rehearsal, ca. 1895. Photograph taken in auditorium of the main building.*

*William Corbin.*

# WHAT IS REQUIRED OF STUDENTS

### IN THE

# OHIO UNIVERSITY.

1. Obedience to the laws of the University, and the authority of its Officers.

2. Diligence and faithful application to study.

3. Regular and punctual attendance on all College duties.

4. To be in their respective rooms during the hours of study, and after 9 o'clock at night, unless leave of absence shall have been obtained.

5. To retire to rest at or before 10 o'clock at night, and in no case, except in sickness or special permission, to have lights burning in rooms after 10 o'clock at night.

6. To keep their rooms neatly and in good order; and to avoid sweeping into the Halls, or throwing from the windows ashes, water, or filth of any kind.

7. To occupy rooms in the College Buildings, unless by permission of the President; and not to remove from the particular rooms assigned them, except by the same permission.

8. To attend College Examinations.

9. To take such part in College Examinations as shall be assigned, and to speak only such matter as shall have been previously approved by the Faculty.

10. To abstain from smoking tobacco in the College Buildings.

11. To respect the Sabbath and religious institutions.

12. To attend reverently the worship of the Chapel, and public worship twice on the Sabbath, including the Lecture in the Chapel on Sabbath afternoon.

13. To avoid profanity, obscenity, and vulgarity.

14. To observe polite and decorous deportment toward each other, and toward all other persons.

15. To observe cleanliness, both as it respects person and dress.

16. To give testimony when called upon by the Faculty, concerning irregularities and transgression of College order.

17. To be responsible for damage done to their respective rooms, and for general damage done where the perpetrator cannot be discovered.

*Rules of Conduct, 1840. Ohio University, Mahn Library Collection.*

*Courtesy of Linda McDowell.*

*J. C. Corbin, third grand master, Arkansas Grand Lodge Prince Hall Masons, Pine Bluff, organized in 1873. Hubbell, Ken PS02-03, Courtesy of the Arkansas State Archives*

*Joseph C. Corbin and public school teachers attending a Normal Institute around 1895. These were short courses for the improvement of teachers in Arkansas. Teachers with the best reputations and qualifications were chosen to conduct normal institutes. On June 10, 1895, a normal institute for black teachers opened at Branch Normal College with an attendance of 42 teachers.*

*Members of Branch Normal College Class of 1888. Pictured are John W. Corbin, Lucinda Alexander, Lawson T. Thomas, J. S. House, Louis Bunn, and William I. Pumphrey.*

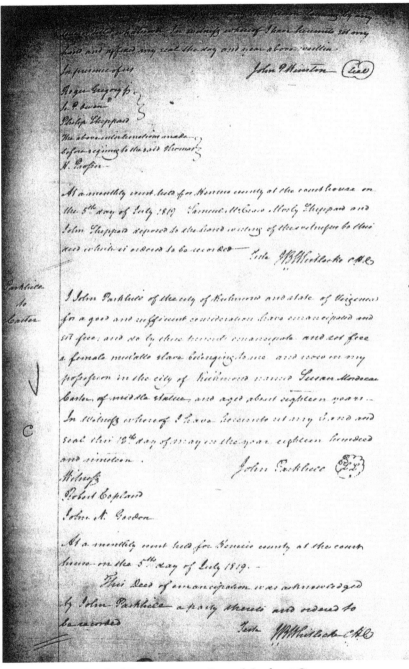

*Deed of Emancipation, Susan Mordecai Carter.*

*John Q. Adams, Corbin's nephew.*

14-1661

## PROBATE DOCKET

33-8968

| | | | Date of Allowance | Class | Amount Allo |
|---|---|---|---|---|---|
| Name of Deceased | *Joseph Carter Corbin* | | ..........191... | | Dollars |
| Date of Death | *Jan 9. 1911* | Claims Allowed—In Whose Favor | | | |
| Name of Executor | *Chicago Title & Trust Co.* | | | | |
| Date of Proof of Will | APR 3 1911 | | | | |
| Name of Administrat | | | | | |
| Date of Letters | APR 3 1911 | | | | |
| Name of Widow | | | | | |
| Names of Heirs | *William Henry Corbin* *Louise Maud* | | | | |
| Amount of Bond | *pursuant to Statute* | | | | |
| Names of Sureties | | | | | |

|  | DATE OF APPROVAL | | |
|---|---|---|---|
| | | Dollars | Cents |
| Inventory | APR 12 1911 | | |
| Appraisement *excused* | APR 12 1911 | | |
| Widow's Award | | | |
| Widow's Selection Filed | | *Hearing on will cont'd to* | |
| Heirship Entered | 1912 | | |
| Adjudication Entered | JUN 5 1911 | | |

### REMARKS AND GENERAL ABSTRACT OF PROCEEDINGS

G 19 1912 *On Pet of Extr Ord it be erased from Reg R.E. under Torrens Act.*

N 6 1913 FINAL ACCOUNT APPROVED FILED & APP DISCHARGED *Costs Pd.*

SETTLED

*Jefferson County probate document on Joseph Carter Corbin.*

COPY

Oberlin College Archives

OBERLIN COLLEGE RECORDS

NAME John Ward Corbin                    Of the Class of _____

PRESENT ADDRESS:                    Former Student, Years 88-90
BUSINESS

RESIDENCE_____

OCCUPATION Died about 1909

IF MARRIED, FULL NAME OF WIFE _____

IF DECEASED, DATE AND PLACE OF DEATH_____

Name of someone who may be able to supply this information, if you are unable to:
NAME City Clerk's Office, City Hall, Little Rock, Ark.,
ADDRESS if the death occurred in the City of Little Rock.
    Otherwise there will be no record of this death,
This card filled out by: NAME as this Bureau was established in 1914.

DATE_____ ADDRESS _____

OBERLIN COLLEGE RECORDS

NAME John Ward Corbin                    Of the Class of _____

PRESENT ADDRESS:                    Former Student, Years 88-90
BUSINESS

RESIDENCE_____

OCCUPATION Died about 1909

IF MARRIED, FULL NAME OF WIFE _____

IF DECEASED, DATE AND PLACE OF DEATH_____

Name of someone who may be able to supply this information, if you are unable to: Thank you.
NAME Bureau of Vital Statistics, State Board of Health
ADDRESS Little Rock, Arkansas

This card filled out by: NAME JEFFERSON COUNTY HEALTH UNIT,
DATE 3/7/33 ADDRESS Pine Bluff, Arkansas

*Oberlin College record on John Ward Corbin.*

Death Certificate of Will Corbin.

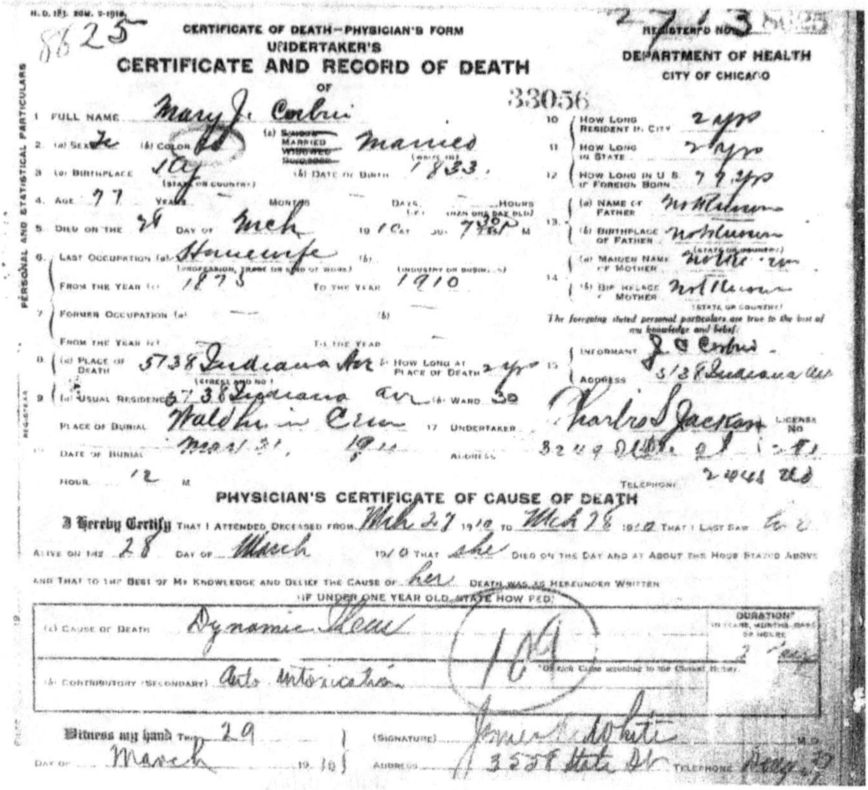

H. D. 181. 20M. 2-1910.

8825

CERTIFICATE OF DEATH—PHYSICIAN'S FORM
UNDERTAKER'S
CERTIFICATE AND RECORD OF DEATH
OF

Registered No. 2713

DEPARTMENT OF HEALTH
CITY OF CHICAGO

33056

PERSONAL AND STATISTICAL PARTICULARS

1 FULL NAME Mary J. Corbin
2 (a) Sex Fe (b) Color (c) Single, Married, Widowed, Divorced Married
3 (a) Birthplace (State or Country) (b) Date of Birth 1833.
4. Age 77 Years Months Days Hours
5. Died on the 28 Day of Mch 1910 at 7 30 P M
6. Last Occupation (a) Housewife (profession, trade or kind of work) (b) (industry or business)
From the Year (c) 1875 To the Year 1910
7 Former Occupation (a) (b)
From the Year (c) To the Year
8 (a) Place of Death 5738 Indiana Av (street and no.) (b) How Long at Place of Death 2 yrs
9 (a) Usual Residence 5738 Indiana av (b) Ward 30
Place of Burial Waldheim Cem
Date of Burial Mar 31, 1910
Hour 12 M
10 How Long Resident in City 2 yrs
11 How Long in State 2 yrs
12 How Long in U.S. if Foreign Born 77 yrs
13 (a) Name of Father not known
(b) Birthplace of Father not known (State or Country)
14 (a) Maiden Name of Mother not known
(b) Birthplace of Mother not known (State or Country)
The foregoing stated personal particulars are true to the best of my knowledge and belief.
15 Informant J. O. Corbin
Address 5738 Indiana av
17 Undertaker Charles S Jackson License No.
Address 3249 State St
Telephone

PHYSICIAN'S CERTIFICATE OF CAUSE OF DEATH

I Hereby Certify That I Attended Deceased from Mch 27 1910 to Mch 28 1910 That I Last Saw her Alive on the 28 Day of March 1910 That she Died on the Day and at About the Hour Stated Above and That to the Best of My Knowledge and Belief the Cause of her Death was as Hereunder Written
(If under one year old, state how fed.)

(a) Cause of Death Dynamic Ileus — Duration 2 days
(b) Contributory (Secondary) Auto intoxication
*Of each Cause according to the Clinical History.

104

Witness my hand This 29 Day of March 1910
(Signature) James White M.D.
Address 3558 State St Telephone Doug. 39

Death Certificate of Mary Jane Corbin.

*W. H. Langford, Board of Trustee member and the appointed overseer of the Branch Normal campus.*

*Effie Stewart's Certificate of Examination, 1892.*

. . . *Rectius . videtur . ingenii . quam . virium opibus . gloriam . quærere* . . . . . . . .

✦ **Class · of · 1891.** ✦

| | |
|---|---|
| Miss GEORGIANA BROWN, | THADDEUS COBB, |
| Miss LUELLA V. PATILLO, | ZACHARY T. WASHINGTON, |
| JOSEPH ROSE, | ROBERT N. DAVIS, |
| ADAM ARRANT, | CHARLES M. NEVILLS, |
| ANDREW COBB, Jr., | REUBEN FAGAN. |
| JOHN H. VICKERS. | |

*Your presence is respectfully requested at the Commencement Exercises, Wednesday Evening, June third, at eight o'clock 1891.*

*Commencement*

· BRANCH · NORMAL · COLLEGE ·
PINE BLUFF, ARK.,
✧ Wednesday, June 3d, 1891. ✧

*Branch Normal College's 1891 Commencement Invitation.*

Return to J. C. CORBIN,
PINE BLUFF, ARKANSAS,
If not delivered within 5 days.

The Milton Bradley Co,
Springfield,
Mass.

*Envelope from Joseph C. Corbin dated April 1896.*

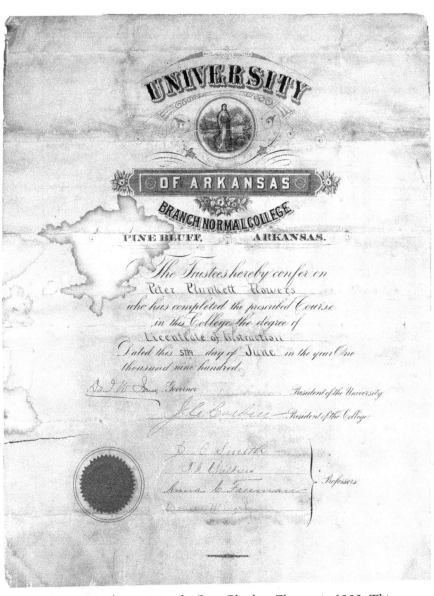

*Licentiate of Instruction for Peter Plunkett Flowers in 1900. This diploma was signed by Joseph C. Corbin.*

tliche Blätter.

Sonntagsblatt
des
mati Volksblattes.

6 F. Hassaurek.....Herausgeber

l, den 16. September 1866.

itischer Wochenbericht.

tump = Tour des Präsidenten
Norden und Westen der loyalen
hat gestern endlich ihr Ende erie war eine degoutirende „Fai-
: selbst die Freunde des Präsi-
ngestehen müssen. Volk und
welche in ihm den obersten Be-

Ver. Staaten ehrerbietig be-
nußten sich durch die rücksichts-
und Weise verletzt fühlen, in
s Compliment überall — durch
Partei = Speeches höchst un-
erwiderte; denn von der Wahr-
on ihm überall aufgestellten,
die Rebellenstaaten nie aus der
esen seien, daß es nie Rebellen-
geben habe, daß die Rebellen-
durch my policy wieder in die
gebracht werden könnten und
welche sich dieser Politik wider-
nionisten und Verräther seien,
ur Wenige oder Niemanden
aben.

richten aus Deutschland lau-
iebigend. Der Friede mit
ar noch nicht abgeschlossen.
rlangt, daß die sächsische Armee
garnisonirt werden und dem
Fahneneid schwören sollen, so-

welcher in Tennessee zu den Farbigen sagte: „Haltet
euch an mich und ich will euer Moses sein und
welcher sich nebenbei als ihr Pharao bewiesen hat,
ehe er durch das rothe Meer ging — hat es jetzt
unternommen, der Moses der demokratischen
Partei auf dem Wege durch die Wüste zu sein,
aber ohne Aussicht auf Erfolg. Er wird sie auf-
brauchen; er ist ein größerer Elephant als Vallan-
bigham oder irgend ein anderer Mann, den sie je
durchzusetzen suchten. Johnson's ursprüngliche
Ansicht über Reconstruktion war, die loyalen
Männer des Südens wieder zuzulassen, er trat da-
mals nicht für unbedingte Repräsentation auf;
aber nunmehr ist er offenbar von der Politik irgend
eines rechtschaffenen Demokraten in den Ver
Staaten abgewichen; er ist ein Unterstützer der
südlichen Verräther; er befürwortet und verlangt
die unmittelbare und unbedingte Zulassung von
Vertretern des Südens in den Congreß. Wir
verlangen, daß sie darein willigen, diese Regierung
nicht wieder aufbrechen zu wollen, und dann wollen wir sie zulassen; sie aber sagen, daß sie nicht
wollen und gleichwohl hereinkommen werden; darum dreht sich die Frage."

☞ Vermählungen. Während der mit
dem gestrigen Tage geschlossenen Woche haben die
folgenden 63 Paare ihre Heirathslicensen in der
Probate Court von Hamilton County herausge-
nommen:

| | | |
|---|---|---|
| August Scherman | mit | Mary Gulow |
| Charles Henke | „ | Mina Brinkschröder |
| G. P. Griffith | „ | Charlotte L. Ellis |
| James L. Wallace | „ | Ellen Lampher |
| Willis W. Winson | „ | Armanda Smith |
| Henry A. Harris | „ | Annie M. Burr |
| Augustus J. Clark | „ | Ellen E. Golden |
| Albert Snyder | „ | Hester A. Hedges |
| George Duvall | „ | Alice Balleh |
| Frank Hausman | „ | Catharina Huber |
| Stanislaus Männer | „ | Wilhelmine Udrh |
| August Brust | „ | Ida Brun |
| Ferdinand Risselbach | „ | Kate Lang |
| Roger R. Moore | „ | Maggie Quinlau |
| Balthasar Gallatin | „ | Francisca Winter |
| Henry R. Moore | „ | Anna Christh |
| James Kelleh | „ | Bridget Lhdon |
| George A. Rimsal | „ | Alice J. Rivers |
| Jacob Herberger | „ | Margaret Gardner |
| Gottlieb Ekard | „ | Christina Biegler |
| John Scherer | „ | Francisca Hoffinger |
| Joseph C. Corbin | „ | Mary J. Ward |

Cincinnati German newspaper showing marriage date of
Joseph Carter Corbin.

Corbin's obituary in the *Appeal, January 14, 1911.*

Special Dispatch to the New-York Times.

LITTLE ROCK, ARK., May 18.—The State Republican Convention met at noon today, to appoint delegates to Philadelphia and elect a new State Central Committee. Judge STEPHENSON, of Helena, was elected President; J. Q. Adams, of Jefferson, Secretary; Senator Clayton, Gov. Hadley, Hons. W. H. Grey, Elesba Baxter, Stephen Wheeler, H. Johnson, O. P. Snyder, H. A. Miller, Thomas V. Rankin, J. M. Johnson, H. H. White and C. J. Searle were elected delegates to Philadelphia. A new Central Committee of fifteen members, with Senator CLAYTON as Chairman, was then appointed. The first resolution adopted, indorses the Administration of President GRANT, and declares him the first choice of the Convention for the nominee of the party. The second extends to Senator CLAYTON the full sympathy of the Republicans of the State for him in the malicious assaults made upon him by enemies of Republicans in the Senate of the United States, and through the public Press; and it expresses unshaken confidence in his patriotism and fidelity to the Republican Party. The third indorses the administration of Gov. HADLEY, and expresses confidence in him as a true Republican. The fourth denounces in unmeasured terms the actions of United States Senator BEN. F. RICE. JOS. BROOKS, JAS. L. HODGES and the minority of the State Central Committee, as disorganizers and traitors, acting for the purpose of disorganizing the Republican Party. The fifth resolution strongly indorses the action of the majority in the State Central Committee as wise and patriotic. The sixth resolution bids those Republicans who are following after the false gods set at Cincinnati, to depart in peace. The Convention was the largest ever assembled in this State, and was characterized by great enthusiasm and almost entire unanimity in all respects. One feature deserving of special mention was the fact that it embraced colored men as well as the leading representative men of the State. The entire number of delegates elected, 350, were present in person. In all particulars the Convention was a grand success.

J. G. R.

Dispatch to the New York Times, May 24, 1872, "Arkansas Liberal Republican Convention."

# PROF. J. C. CORBIN IS FOUND DEAD

### Noted Negro Educator Dies Suddenly in This City—Former State Superintendent of Public Instruction.

Joseph Carter Corbin, a highly esteemed and able negro educator, was found dead at his home, No. 1821 West Second avenue, yesterday morning at 9 o'clock by members of his family. The body had all appearances of his coming to his death from natural causes. He was seventy-five years old and a native of Chillicothe, Ohio.

Members of Prof. Corbin's family attempted to arouse him at 9 o'clock when he was found dead in bed. Dr. B. H. Galligher was called to attend him but life was pronounced extinct. Coroner H. E. Williams was then called to look into the case. The Coroner said death was due to natural causes and an inquest was not held.

The deceased is survived by a son, Will Corbin of this city, and a daughter, Louisa M. Corbin, of East St. Louis, Ill. With the funeral arrangements not yet completed the body lies in state at Holderness' undertaking establishment. The remains will probably be taken to Chicago for interment.

The dead negro educator has been regarded as one of the most learned of his race in the south, and has even been compared with Booker T. Washington by his intimate friends. He was a graduate of Ohio University. Prof. Corbin was well known throughout this state and the south on account of the important positions he has held during his career. He was distinguished by official positions in the postal service in this state and high positions as an educator of negroes. The most brilliant accomplishment of the dead educator in this state was his establishment of and presiding over the Branch Normal College in this city for thirty years.

Prof. Corbin was a grand trustee of the Masonic Temple fund of the Colored Masonic lodge in this city, and he was also a prominent member of the lodge. He was elected state superintendent of public instruction in 1870 on the Baxter ticket.

Prof. Isaac Fisher of the Branch Normal College has issued a letter to the relatives of the deceased negro, stating that out of respect to Prof. Corbin, who lent so much aid to the Branch Normal College, the students of the institution wish to hold the memorial services in the chapel of the college buildings.

Pine Bluff Daily Graphic, *January 10, 1911.*

## Arkansas Republican Convention No. 1.

LITTLE ROCK, ARK., July 23.—The Republican State Convention adjourned to-day. The following are the nominations for State officers: Governor—A. W. Bishop; Secretary of State—W. L. Copeland (colored); Treasurer—A. A. C. Rogers; Auditor—J. R. Berry; Attorney General—H. A. Pierce; Land Commissioner—R. W. McDonald; School Superintendent—J. C. Corbin (colored); Chancellor—Lafayette Gregg; Chancery Clerk—J. T. White (colored).

The resolutions adopted indorse the National Republican ticket, the one-term principle, and Civil Service reform as recommended by Governor Hayes; declare the Republican party, in elevating to citizenship the colored race, entitled to continued confidence; demand civil and political recognition of all men; proclaim that the present party now administering the State Government is without a platform or financial or governmental policy, and its tendency reactionary; oppose repudiation of any indebtedness found to have been legally contracted; favor free schools and reduction of taxes. A resolution was also adopted inviting co-operation of the Liberal Democrats. The State Central Committee was authorized to confer with the State Convention, which meets on the 9th of August, and see if there can not be an adjustment of differences between the two wings of the Republican party in this State. An Electoral ticket was also nominated.

*Special Dispatch to the* New York Times, *Arkansas Republican State Convention nominations.*

*Joseph Carter Corbin headstone, 2013, Forest Home Cemetery, Forest Park, Illinois. Courtesy of Gladys Turner Finney.*

*Mary Jane, John W., and William H. Corbin headstone, 2013, Forest Home Cemetery, Forest Park, Illinois. Courtesy Gladys Turner Finney.*

## Citation
### Dr. Joseph Carter Corbin

**Whereas,** Arkansas is blessed with an abundance of citizens whose life experiences provide a wealth of wisdom that serves to guide and influence our state on the road of continual progress; and,

**Whereas,** Dr. Joseph Carter Corbin, whose lifework is now honored with the erection of a Memorial Headstone, was a prominent historic figure in Arkansas education and his legacy to the State of Arkansas lives on in public education and in the University of Arkansas at Pine Bluff, which he founded in 1875; and,

**Whereas,** the House of Representatives of the Eighty-Ninth General Assembly of the State of Arkansas takes great pride in recognizing Dr. Joseph Carter Corbin's Memorial Headstone Dedication and his legacy.

Now therefore, pursuant to the motion of
Representative Mike Holcomb

The Arkansas House of Representatives directs that this Citation be presented on this 27th Day of May, 2013.

_____
SPEAKER OF THE HOUSE

_____
REPRESENTATIVE

*Citations: Arkansas House of Representative, Mike Holcomb.*

## MOST WORSHIPFUL PRINCE HALL GRAND LODGE
### F. & A.M. Jurisdiction of Arkansas
### Organized 1873

**DEPUTY GRAND MASTER**
Walter L. May
P.O. Box 4017
Little Rock, AR 72214
Phone: (501) 912-6122

**SENIOR GRAND WARDEN**
Mark A. McGraw
6822 Marguerite Lane
Little Rock, AR 72205
Phone: (501) 960-2405

**JUNIOR GRAND WARDEN**
Brian Johnson
10 Beauregard Drive
Little Rock, AR 72206
Phone: (501) 519-3702

**GRAND SECRETARY**
Thomas W. Brown, Sr.
P.O. Box 403
Elaine, AR 72333
Phone: (870) 817-2162
Email: prihglo@cablelynx.com

2906 East Harding Avenue
Pine Bluff, Arkansas 71601
Office Phone: (870) 534-5467
Toll Free (Arkansas ONLY): 1-800-265-3295

**Cleveland K. Wilson Grand Master**
P.O. Box 492
Hamburg, AR 71646
Phone (Cell) 870-853-6634
Fax: (870)535-3581

**GRAND TREASURER**
John L. Colbert
2140 Loren Circle
Fayetteville, AR 72701
Phone: (479) 521-2399

**SEC/TREAS. RELIEF**
Edward C. Beale, II
1003 Chepstow Lane
Sherwood, AR 72120
Phone: (479)521-2399

**ASST. SEC/TREAS. RELIEF**
Richard Richardson
213 Falcon Cove
White Hall, AR 71662
Phone: (870) 489-2599

**C.C.F.C**
William J. Bryant
2103 Wellington Drive
Pine Bluff, AR 71603
Phone: (501) 968-2405

Whereas J.C. Corbin served the Jurisdiction of Arkansas as the third Grand Master: and

Whereas he organized the Grand Chapter of the Order of the Eastern Star in 1885, and

Whereas he served the Grand Chapter of the Order of the Eastern Star as its first Secretary; and

Whereas he was involved in organizing other houses of freemasonry; and

Whereas he was an educational leader in the jurisdiction,

Whereas we feel that this act of appreciation is fitting for such a man; therefore, be it resolved by The Most Worshipful Prince Hall Grand Lodge of Arkansas, Free and Accepted Masons with humble submission thank him again post-humously for his many contributions to Prince Hall Masonry.

Be it further, resolved that a copy of this Resolution be given to the family this day, May 27, 2013; and a copy be placed in the historical archives.

Cleveland K. Wilson
Grand Master

Attest:

Thomas W. Brown
Grand Secretary

*"Teamwork and Brotherhood"*

*Most Worshipful Prince Hall Grand Lodge of Arkansas Resolution on Dedication of Memorial Headstone for Dr. Joseph Carter Corbin, Memorial Day, May 27, 2013.*

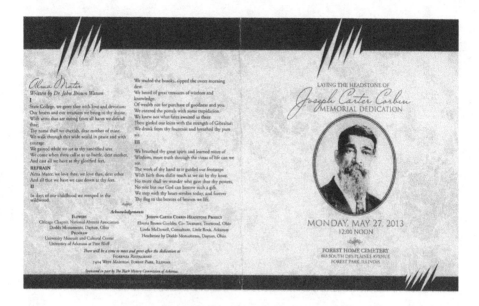

## Biography

Joseph Carter Corbin, American Educator, Linguist, Mathematician, Musician, Scholar, was born March 26, 1833 to William and Susan Corbin at Chillicothe, Ohio. A distinguished graduate of Ohio University, where he received a B.A. degree in Art in 1853, and two master's degrees, (1856, 1859).

He was elected Arkansas State Superintendent of Public Education in 1872. While in this position, he served as Chairman of the Board of the newly-formed Arkansas Industrial University (now the University of Arkansas at Fayetteville), and recommended a "college for the education of the poorer classes."

In, 1875, Corbin became founder and principal of Branch Normal College (now the University of Arkansas at Pine Bluff) where he served until 1902. He then became principal of Merrill High School. He was co-founder of Teachers of Negro Youth in Arkansas with fellow educator, Professor Rufus C. Childress, the first black state teachers' organization, and was its first president. Professor Corbin was a leader in the public education movement in Arkansas.

Joseph Carter Corbin was married to Mary Jane Ward of Louisville, Kentucky on September 11, 1866. To this union six children were born. Among them were John W. Corbin, William H. Corbin, Fauolina Corbin, Pea Corbin, and Louisa Corbin.

He was a leader in the Prince Hall Masons. He was Grand Secretary for twenty-five years, and the fourth Grand Master of the Most Worshipful Prince Hall Grand Lodge of Free and Accepted Masons of Arkansas. He authored The Status of Colored Freemasons in 1896.

His wife and four children predeceased Professor Corbin. Professor Corbin died January 9, 1911 in Pine Bluff. He was interred January 14, 1911 at Waldheim German Cemetery (now Forest Home), Forest Park, Illinois. He is buried alongside his wife, Mary Jane and sons, John and William Corbin.

## Order of Program

PRAYER
Miss Christine Parker, '74
Chicago Alumni Chapter, UAPB

INTRODUCTION AND REMARKS
Dr. Gladys Turner Finney '57, Presiding
Chairperson
Joseph Carter Corbin Headstone Project,
Dayton, Ohio

GREETINGS
Ms. Henri Linton, Sr., Director
University Museum and Cultural Center,
University of Arkansas at Pine Bluff,
Pine Bluff Arkansas

THE OCCASION
Mr. Tony Burroughs, FUGA
Genealogist-Author
Chicago, Illinois

SPEAKER
The Honorable
Congressman Danny Davis, '61
Illinois 7th Congressional District
U.S. House of Representatives

LAYING OF UAPB WREATH
Ms. Jockey Caton '65, President
Chicago Chapter, National Alumni
Association, Dr. Gladys Turner Finney

LAYING OF MASONIC WREATH
Mr. Frederick McNeal, Jr. '71
Most Worshipful Prince Hall
Grand Lodge, State of Illinois

PROCLAMATION
The Honorable
Anthony Calderone, Mayor
Forest Park, Illinois

AUDIENCE COMMENTS

ACKNOWLEDGEMENTS
Dr. Gladys Turner Finney

BENEDICTION
Mrs. Carla Coleman, Chair
The Black History Commission of Arkansas

ALMA MATER

Program from the Joseph Carter Corbin Memorial Headstone dedication.

*Certificate of Recognition*

*Presented to*

# Joseph Carter Corbin Headstone Project

Please allow me to extend my sincere thanks and congratulations to the Joseph Carter Corbin Headstone Project as you commemorate the Memorial Headstone Dedication for Dr. Joseph Carter Corbin.

I am proud to join you in recognizing the accomplishments of this esteemed Ohioan. As the founder and president of the first African-American institution of higher education in Arkansas, Dr. Corbin broke barriers and laid the foundations for future educational and racial reforms.

Thank you for your efforts to ensure that Dr. Corbin's legacy is not forgotten.

Sincerely,

*Sherrod Brown*

Sherrod Brown
United States Senator

May 27, 2013

*Certificate of Recognition: United States Senate—Ohio senator Sherrod Brown.*

# In the name and by the Authority of
# THE STATE OF OHIO

## John R. Kasich

*Governor of Ohio*

*hereby officially recognizes*

### THE DEDICATION CEREMONY OF
# JOSEPH CARTER CORBIN'S
# HEADSTONE

Born in Chillicothe, Ohio, Joseph Carter Corbin solidified his role in history as an American Educator, scholar, linguist, mathematician, and musician. Although he is one of Ohio University's most notable alumni, Corbin established his legacy in Arkansas where he was an advocate for quality public education. For this reason, you are gathered today to celebrate the dedication of his headstone, and pay tribute to the great work he accomplished throughout his life. I commend each and every individual who put their time and effort toward orchestrating this event.

Best wishes for a safe and memorable event!

On this 27th day of May, 2013

John R. Kasich
Governor

*Tribute by Ohio governor Kasich on dedication of Memorial Headstone for Dr. Joseph Carter Corbin, Memorial Day, May 27, 2013.*

*Resolution: Mayor's Office, Forest Park, Illinois. Photo is of Mayor Calderone and Dr. Gladys Turner Finney accepting the resolution.*

*St. Paul Missionary Baptist Church cornerstone.*

## CHAPTER 10

# Corbin's Dimensions

In *Two Centuries of Methodist Concern, Bondage, Freedom and Education of Black People*, James P. Brawley cited eight dimensions early teachers and administrators of historically black colleges possessed: preparedness, dedication, sacrifice, love, a sense of mission, identification, leadership, and personality impact.[1] Professor Corbin brought all these dimensions to Branch Normal College.

**Preparedness:** Professor Corbin received a strong education in the North at Ohio University. He came to the South and gave his best, intellectually and culturally, to the cause of educating African Americans in Arkansas.

**Dedication:** Professor Corbin was dedicated beyond measure. For seven years, 1875 to 1882, he was the only teacher at Branch Normal College. He was an accomplished musician. He played and taught students to play piano, organ, and flute, and he trained the Normal School choir, which was featured at each commencement.[2] He was the organizer and conductor of the first choir and first band at Branch Normal College.

**Sacrifice:** Professor Corbin served Branch Normal College for nearly three decades, under the administration of ten governors of Arkansas.

**Love:** It was Professor Corbin's love for his profession, the cause, and the people of Arkansas who needed his help that gave his life meaning.

**Sense of Mission:** No challenge—inadequate funding, condition of the students, or external interference—could alter his sense of mission. Education was part of his value system and inherent to his life's meaning and work.

**Identification:** Professor Corbin was identified with the great cause of educating a people who had been denied education under slavery. This undoubtedly gave fulfillment and satisfaction to his labors. Because of Professor Corbin and Branch Normal, Arkansas African Americans received a college degree. Large numbers were prepared as teachers and, as historian Robert A. Leflar put it, "sent forth to educate others all over the state."[3]

**Leadership:** Governor Simon Pollard Hughes Jr. in his message to the Arkansas State Legislature on January 12, 1887, said of Professor Corbin: "I call attention, with pleasure, to the favorable mention of the efficient and faithful management of the Normal Branch of the University of Pine Bluff by Professor Corbin, in the report of the Executive Committee of the Board of Trustees." He added his own commendations of Professor Corbin as an "able and efficient principal of that school, devoted to its interest, successful in its management, which has been very careful and economical."[4]

**Personality Impact:** The African American people needed inspiration and were inspired by people like Professor Corbin.

According to author William J. Simmons, "He had that rare gift of making others pleased with themselves. He was a man of fine personal qualities, retiring in his nature and very modest."[5] He created within the students a desire to learn and to be somebody.

A moving tribute to Professor Corbin regarding a former student, Joseph A. Booker, is found in E. M. Woods's *Blue Book of Little Rock and Argenta*. Booker became a minister, educator, and president of Arkansas Baptist College:

> At the age of nineteen, in the year 1878, [Booker] left the farm and home people to enter Branch Normal at Pine Bluff, Arkansas. There a new horizon presented itself to him. There he got a larger view of education. For while he left home, as he told his people, to review his education, and while he supposed it would take him six months to review, he soon found that he had no education to review. His teacher, Professor Joseph C. Corbin, principal of Branch Normal College, soon created in him a thirst for deep and intricate learning. He spent three years under this teacher and in this school."[6]

A Joint Committee of the Arkansas House and Senate in 1891 described Professor Corbin as "a very zealous and successful teacher who commanded the utmost respect, not only from all his pupils and teachers, but from all the citizens of Pine Bluff."[7]

## Advocate for the Students

Professor Corbin's compassion for the economic plight of his students caused him to protest against, as he said, a "rigid collection of tuition fees because our people have been impoverished, and a rigid insistence would have depleted the school." He regarded it as a "matter of absolute impossibility to comply with the regulations regulating appointments." He thought "the entire system should be abolished, that a small monthly fee should be collected or the institution made absolutely free." He reminded the Board of Trustees that Branch Normal College had been explicitly established for the benefit of the poorer classes and he had been "much grieved to refuse some poor fellows who came from distant counties because they were unable to pay down the five dollars' entrance fee."[8]

"In venturing to offer these suggestions to your Honorable Body," Professor Corbin wrote in his Narrative Report to the Board of Trustees, "I have been guided by my knowledge of the extreme poverty of many of my students, which is a real stubborn fact, admitting of no doubt...I have no doubt of there being students at the University, but they are a small minority; at this institution, they are the great majority. I sympathize very strongly with them; because I have experienced the very same difficulties, and know by actual experiences the disadvantages of extreme poverty."[9] Professor Corbin advocated compensation for students who assisted him. He recommended the hiring of James Smith, the first collegiate graduate of Branch Normal College.

The multi-dimensional Professor Corbin was also able to use his hands to perform many tasks required by Branch Normal College. He cleared away the forest, burned the brush, and chopped the trees for fuel. He was both principal and janitor. "Putting the apparatus in 'knock down shape' into proper condition was done almost entirely by the unaided labor of the Principal. He assisted in putting up the machinery in the shops with the aid of the students. He assisted in making the calculations necessary in properly adjusting the revolving machinery in the shops. He built with own hands a back porch, and some chicken houses in the rear of the dormitory for the convenience of the women students."[10] He was willing to do anything in his power to aid the success of Branch Normal College.

100

## Scholarly Works

Professor Corbin was one of the most scholarly men of his day, as a mathematician, scholar, and linguist—fluent in Greek, Latin, German, French, Spanish, and Italian. Documents of his day are not easily obtained, however, as many have not been kept. His mathematical solutions appeared in *Barnes' Educational Monthly*, the *School Visitor*, the *Mathematical Visitor*, the *Mathematical Magazine*, and the *Mathematical Gazette*.

The *Barnes' Educational Monthly*, published in New York, could not be found, as it is no longer in publication. The *School Visitor* was published between 1800 and 1880 in Gettysburg, Ohio. The Miami University Library at Oxford, Ohio, had eight originals of the sixteen volumes in their Special Collections. Professor Corbin was a regular contributor to this journal. The *Mathematical Magazine* was published in Erie, Pennsylvania, between 1882 and 1910. Oberlin College Library held copies of the *Mathematical Magazine* and the *Mathematical Monthly*.

## Secondary Education

Professor Corbin conducted training institutes during the summer for public school teachers throughout the state under the State Superintendent of Education to demonstrate teaching methods and improve teacher effectiveness. He was also the Jefferson County Teacher Examiner for Colored Teachers. In his Narrative Report to Governor Miller and the Arkansas Industrial University for the school year ending June 14, 1878, Corbin reported that he had issued "one first, nine second, and four third-grade certificates of the school."

Professor Corbin was co-founder—along with fellow educator Rufus C. Childress—of the Arkansas Teachers Association

(ATA) in 1898; he was also its first president. The ATA was founded in Pine Bluff with fewer than a dozen teachers of black children. Long after, in 1969, the ATA merged with the formerly all-white Arkansas Education Association. Corbin also held membership in the National Education Association and the National Commission for Promotion of Universities of the United States.[11]

Corbin's colleague Professor Childress was a prominent and well-known educator for whom Childress Hall on the campus of AM&N College was named to commemorate his profound impact upon education in the state. Childress had the distinction of being a Rosenwald Building Agent, and, under his supervision, nearly 400 schools were constructed in Arkansas at a cost of over two million dollars. Professor Childress served as Assistant Supervisor of Negro Education for the state. He also organized the first Arkansas branch of the Congress of Colored Parents and Teachers.[12] Today, Childress Hall houses the University of Arkansas at Pine Bluff Museum and Cultural Center.

## Corbin and Prince Hall Free and Accepted Masons

Professor Corbin was the third grand master of the Most Worshipful Prince Hall Grand Lodge of Arkansas, which was organized in 1873. He was elected Grand Master in 1878 and served three terms. For twenty-seven years, he served as Grand Secretary and was also Foreign Correspondent. He was a commander in the Knights Templar. He organized the Grand Chapter of the Order of the Eastern Star in 1885 and served as its first secretary.[13] Corbin was an account holder, as secretary of the Grand Lodge of Arkansas, in the Freedman's Bank, Little Rock.[14] The Masonic Temple, located at Fourth Avenue and State Street, in Pine Bluff, was built by and for the Grand Lodge of Arkansas. When completed in 1904, it was the tallest building in Pine Bluff. Over a thousand masons attended the cornerstone-laying ceremony in 1902. The stone was donated by the Grand Chapter Order of the Eastern Star. The *Pine Bluff Commercial* characterized it as an "impressive building with arched window openings on the top floor and rusticated stone columns at the storefront."[15] Many of the city's professionals and businessmen had their offices and retail stores there. Corbin's name was etched on the cornerstone as Grand Secretary and Secretary of the Board of Trustees. Corbin authored *The Status of Colored Freemasons* in 1896 and *Minutes of Masonry, Grand Lodge of Arkansas, 1873 to 1902.*[16]

## Religious Affiliation

Joseph Carter Corbin was affiliated with the Union Baptist Church of Cincinnati. The church was founded July 14, 1831, and its first pastor was the Reverend David Leroy Nickens of Chillicothe, Ohio. It is the oldest African American Baptist church in Cincinnati with the oldest Baptist cemetery. Corbin was active in the leadership of Union Baptist Church. According to Union Baptist Church Minutes, April 26, 1864, to September 5, 1866, Corbin served as clerk, was appointed clerk pro tem, was elected trustee, and served on the committee on hymn books. The *African American National Biography*, quoting the September 24, 1864, Union Baptist Church Minutes, said, "Corbin is an accomplished musician [and] directed the choir at the dedication of Union Baptist Church."[17]

Union Baptist Cemetery was founded in 1864. Pre– and post–Civil War records that remain of the Union Baptist Church are archived at the John Parker Research Library at the Cincinnati Underground Railroad Freedom Center.

Professor Corbin's daughter, Faustina Corbin, was reinterred at Union Baptist Cemetery from Oakland Cemetery, Little Rock, Arkansas. Professor Corbin's parents and his sister, Elizabeth Corbin, were buried at Union Baptist Cemetery. Elizabeth Corbin's funeral was held at Mound Street Church in 1893. The author was unable to locate the graves of Corbin's parents, siblings, or daughter at Union Baptist Cemetery. A notice on the cemetery's website states, "No official records are known to exist prior to 1884 other than the gravestones."[18] Many of the cemetery records were lost in a fire.

## Community Service

Professor Corbin was civic-minded. He was vice president of the Colored Industrial Fair Association of Pine Bluff.[19] A group of prominent black Arkansas business and political leaders, including Corbin, organized the Arkansas branches of the National Negro Business League.[20] He was an active member of the Pine Bluff Immigration Bureau, which included L. Altheimer, S. Geisreiter, and Wiley Jones.[21]

CHAPTER 11:

# Social Status

Much has been written about the "aristocrats of color" and "the black elite" during the nineteenth and early twentieth centuries. "Aristocrats of color" was a term used to describe the black upper class. Although there is no evidence Professor Corbin ever regarded himself as such, he fit the profile due to his education, extraordinary achievement, and prominence in the social life of his community.

Aristocrats of color lived in black communities, large and small, throughout the United States, and their capital was Washington DC, according to Professor Willard B. Gatewood in his book *Aristocrats of Color: The Black Elite, 1880–1920*. Divided into two strata, there were the "old families" who were the top tier and the newcomers' second tier. A small group of black citizens stood at the top of the pyramid. They were light in complexion, and their style of living more closely resembled the "better class of whites." According to Gatewood,

> Having acquired the first higher education and produced the earliest black professionals, they were community leaders,

lived in the best houses, and spent their money on travel, books, musical instruments, and education of their children. They felt a responsibility to the less fortunate but had little contact with or knowledge of lower class blacks.[1]

Aristocrats of color supported causes and organizations that benefited the race. Holding status as free persons in the antebellum South and having mixed ancestry with white families were also common elements of this black elite. Gatewood explained:

> In the Black communities of St. Paul and Minneapolis where there was a high correlation between light skin and social prominence, an aristocracy of a dozen persons dominated intellectual, social, and political life. Among them was John Q. Adams: "an Oberlin graduate and newspaper publisher who figured prominently in various civil rights causes. Adams was the scion of an old and prominent black family in Louisville, Kentucky." He was active for a time in Reconstruction politics in Arkansas, where his Uncle Joseph C. Corbin achieved prominence as a politician and educator.[2]

Professor Corbin was a contemporary of Ferdinand Havis and Wiley Jones of Pine Bluff. All three were Republicans and Prince Hall Masons. Havis was elected to the Arkansas House of Representatives in 1872, the same year Corbin was elected State Superintendent of Public Instruction. Havis also held county and local public office as Jefferson County Assessor and Alderman of the Third Ward. Wiley Jones, a former slave, was a successful businessman and considered the "richest colored man in America" according to *Men of Mark*.[3]

Corbin was a fellow student in subscription schools with John Mercer Langston in Chillicothe, Ohio. P. B. S. Pinchback and John Mercer Langston attended the Reverend Gilmore's High School in Cincinnati. Langston became a lawyer and dean of the Law School at Howard University. He was also minister to Haiti, and chargé d'affaires to the Dominican Republic.[4] Corbin would likely have known Pinchback of Louisiana, as his brother, Henry A. Corbin, was Pinchback's private secretary when Pinchback was lieutenant governor of Louisiana. Corbin also knew the Reverend William J. Simmons, who "was examined and secured a State teaching certificate from the Honorable Superintendent of Education, J. C. Corbin."[5]

Mentioned briefly by Gatewood was Corbin's nephew Cyrus Field Adams. Adams was a successful Chicago businessman and co-editor of the *Appeal* newspaper with his brother, John Q. Adams. Cyrus Adams gained prominence in Republican politics and was assistant register of the United States Treasury. He was also an author, teacher, historian, and linguist. As part of the black elite, he was publicly accused by blacks of trying to pass for white. Both of Corbin's nephews achieved the status of aristocrats of color.

Professor Corbin's social status as an educator and head of Branch Normal College would have placed him on equal rank with those designated as the black elite. He would have been welcomed into their ranks and held in high regard. He would have been held in high esteem by the greater African American community as well. While Professor Corbin is not labeled an aristocrat of color by Gatewood, Corbin embodied these characteristics.

## CHAPTER 12

# A Journey of More than
# a Quarter Century Ends

P rofessor Joseph Carter Corbin's long career at Branch Normal College came to an end in 1902 after twenty-seven years of dedicated service to the school. He was not fired by an official action of the Board of Trustees. In fact, the Board of Trustees' Minutes are conspicuous in their failure to mention Professor Corbin's departure. But the board did not have to fire him. All power over the staff had been relegated, by the board, to Trustee William Langford, who served as the board's agent. After losing his appeal for reinstatement, Professor Corbin became principal of Merrill High School in Pine Bluff.

Isaac Fisher, Professor Corbin's successor, gives some insight as to why Professor Corbin was eventually removed. From 1893 to 1902, after his demotion as administrator of Branch Normal College, Professor Corbin no doubt held a tenuous relationship with William Stephen Harris, who was treasurer and superintendent of shops. Corbin disapproved of Harris's management of the college on a cash basis and suspected Harris of immoral behavior toward female students. Corbin at first seemed to attempt a good relationship with Harris. In Corbin's 1893 Narrative Report, for example, he described the relationship with Treasurer Harris and his assistant regarding the Mechanical Department as "agreeable and harmonious as they had shown great and intelligent interest in its working."[1] But in a letter to Professor Booker T. Washington, dated October 10, 1902, Corbin's successor, Professor Fisher, stated: "Our Treasurer, who is a white man is not popular with the Negroes of this town because it is felt that he is immoral and that he has debauched several of the students of this school. It was claimed that the former principal was deposed because he took cognizance of certain immoral relations said to exist between this man [Harris] and a student."[2]

In 1915, Harris touched off the most dramatic incident in Branch Normal College history when he insulted a female freshman student, Miss Ophelia Wade, by giving her a pair of silk stockings. In protest, the students went on strike. The governor then closed the school and promised an investigation. The black community was outraged and sent a delegation and petition to the governor by some of its well-known citizens.

## CHAPTER 13

# Death and Estate

P rofessor Corbin died on January 9, 1911, of heart failure at his residence in Pine Bluff. He was seventy-seven years old. He was survived by his daughter Louisa Maude Corbin of East St. Louis, Illinois, and his son William (Will) Corbin of Pine Bluff.

Notices of his death were carried in the *Pine Bluff Graphics*, the *Pine Bluff Commercial*, the *Appeal*, the *Arkansas Gazette*, the *East St. Louis Journal*, and the *Mathematical Monthly*. His body lay for viewing at H. I. Holderness Undertakers and was shipped to Chicago for burial at the German Waldheim Cemetery at Forest Park, Illinois. The H. I. Holderness Company was a white funeral home located at 301 West Second Avenue and owned by Harry Iverson Holderness. Holderness was later a three-time mayor of Pine Bluff, and he was a member of the Board of Trustees of AM&N College for twenty years. Holderness Hall, a dormitory for men built on the campus in 1939, was named in his honor. The Holderness funeral home became the Holderness-South Mortuary, and today is known as the Fuller Hale-South Funeral Service.[1]

Professor Corbin was interred on January 14, 1911. There was no account of his final burial ceremony, and over the past century his burial site had appeared lost to history until rediscovered by this researcher.

Corbin's successor at Branch Normal College, Professor Isaac Fisher, expressed the sentiment of the students to hold a memorial service for Professor Corbin in the chapel; however, there was no evidence that a memorial service was held on campus or elsewhere in the community. The *Pine Bluff Commercial* reported that Professor Fisher sent a letter of condolences to Corbin's family.[2]

The publishers of the *Appeal*, Corbin's nephews John Q. and Cyrus F. Adams, reported that Professor Corbin was "the last of the Corbin family of Cincinnati, Ohio. This family was held in the highest esteem by all who knew them…and was second to none in the Queen City in point of moral worth, education, general ability, pleasing appearance, and personality."[3]

The *Appeal* reported that at the time of Professor Corbin's death, he "was conducting a high grade correspondence school." The article also noted that Professor Corbin "managed to save some of his earnings and was the possessor of considerable property in Arkansas and Illinois."[4]

Professor Corbin's burial at the German Waldheim Cemetery was by desire and design. He fully intended to be buried there alongside his wife. This was his last wish in his will. A family plot of six graves was purchased at a cost of $125 by Professor Corbin on August 3, 1909.[5] John Ward Corbin, the older son, was the first to be buried there, in 1909, followed by Mrs. Corbin in 1910, Corbin himself in 1911, and William Corbin in 1929. Professor Corbin and his two sons died in Arkansas. Mrs. Corbin died in Chicago. The final resting places of Pea and Louisa M. Corbin are unknown.

The German Waldheim Cemetery dates back to 1873 as a non-religious cemetery for German-speaking immigrants to Chicago. According to a history of the cemetery, "The labor activists executed for their alleged role in the 1886 Haymarket Square bombing are buried here; their striking grave monument has become a magnet for labor leaders, activists, and anarchists from around the world." It merged in 1968 with the Forest Home Cemetery.[6]

Discriminatory burial practices in Chicago were widespread. According to *Chicago Graveyards*, "Price differentials were so common...that in 1911, Edward Green, a Negro member of the state legislature, secured passage of an amendment to the civil rights laws forbidding discriminatory rates in the sale of cemetery plots." As late as 1962, "lily-white cemeteries in the Chicago area were challenged in a court suit by a leading Southside Funeral Director, Marshall F. Bynum, of the Charles S. Jackson Funeral Home."[7]

Mrs. Corbin may have been in Chicago longer than the two years reported on her death certificate. The June 1900 Chicago Census showed Mrs. Corbin in the home of her son, William H. (Will) Corbin, who was head of household, age thirty. His brother, John W., and sister, Louisa Maude Corbin, were also enumerated in the household. Some researchers have suggested that the political climate at the time in Arkansas may have caused her to reside in Chicago.

The two surviving children in 1911 at the time of Professor Corbin's death, Will Corbin and Louisa M. Corbin, were the sole heirs to his estate. The Cotton Belt Savings and Trust Company of Pine Bluff was the executor of the estate. The Executor's Bond was $9,000. The Honorable C. M. Philpot was the Probate Court Judge.[8]

Professor Corbin's home at 1821 West 2nd Avenue in Pine Bluff, two rental houses in Little Rock, furnishings, and cash on hand were valued at $12,783.32. On deposit at the Cotton Belt Savings and Trust was a stock certificate (value not stated) in the American B. Loan Association of Little Rock. There was no debt against the estate except for funeral expenses. The executor made monthly disbursement allowances to William H. and Louisa M. Corbin. The two pieces of real estate in Little Rock at 1407 and 1411 West 6th Street were managed by England Realty Company. Both houses were in walking distance of the Arkansas State Capitol.[9]

The Estate Inventory suggested a life of simplicity but rich in musical instruments—a piano, reed organ, guitar, and mandolin. On July 7, 1911, the executor paid the funeral expenses, which included five regular carriages and two special carriages. This suggests that others were present at the interment in Forest Park, Illinois, besides the two surviving children.

On September 4, 1928, a successor trustee, the Cotton Belt Bank & Trust Company, was assigned, "to receive and collect all funds due the estate and distribute according to the last will and testament of J. C. Corbin, deceased, and render to the court an accounting." On November 27, 1926, the Cotton Belt Savings and Trust Company "ceased to exist as a corporation, and the affairs of said corporation were taken over by the Cotton Belt Bank & Trust Company duly organized under the laws of the State of Arkansas and duly empowered to act as executor and administrator of estates."[10]

Professor Corbin owned property and maintained residences in the South Town Township of Chicago. The executor of his Chicago estate was the Chicago Title and Trust Company. The Cook County, Illinois, Probate Court records were lost. Only the Illinois Probate Court Docket was available, which listed William Henry Corbin and Louisa Maude Corbin as heirs. This will was filed April 3, 1911, and the final settlement date was January 6, 1913.

## CHAPTER 14

# Timeline: Joseph Carter Corbin

Slavery *1619-1864*

**March 26, 1833**—Born free, Chillicothe, Ross County, Ohio

**1848**—Assistant Teacher at Reverend Henry Adams School, Louisville, Kentucky

**Fall, 1850**—Entered Ohio University, Athens, Ohio

**Spring, 1853**—Third Black Student to Graduate from Ohio University, B.A.

**1856**—M.A. Ohio University

**1860**—Employed as Bank Clerk, Ohio Valley Bank, Cincinnati, Ohio

**1861**—Employed as Messenger, Cincinnati

**1863–1869**—Editor and Co-Publisher of the *Colored Citizen* newspaper, Cincinnati

**1864–1865**—Member, Board of Trustees, Cincinnati Colored School Board

## Reconstruction *1865–1877*

**Sept. 16, 1866**—Married Mary Jane Ward, Cincinnati, Ohio

**1868**—Employed as Messenger. Residence: 291 West 3rd Street, Cincinnati

**1870**—Employed as Bank Clerk. Residence: 293 John Street, Cincinnati

**June, 1870**—Elected Trustee of the Cincinnati Colored School Board

**1871**—Moved to Arkansas
Reporter for *Daily Republican*, Powell Clayton's newspaper
Assistant Postmaster at Little Rock, Arkansas

**Oct. 6, 1871**—Secretary for the Organizational Meeting of the Arkansas State Council of the Union League of America (charter granted to Senator Powell Clayton, Governor O. A. Hadley, etc., from National Council)

**1872**—Arkansas Republican State Convention Secretary, Republican Candidate, Arkansas Superintendent of Public Instruction/Public Schools

**Jan. 4, 1873**—Took Office as State Superintendent of Public Instruction/Public Schools

**Jan. 6, 1873–Oct. 30, 1874**—Ex-officio President of Board of Trustees, Arkansas Industrial University (now the University of Arkansas, Fayetteville).
Helped lay foundation for Branch Normal College (now the University of Arkansas at Pine Bluff). Signed contract for construction of University Hall (Old Main), the first building at the University of Arkansas, Fayetteville.

**1874**—Professor of Mathematics, Lincoln Institute, Jefferson City, Missouri

**Aug. 18, 1875**—Hired as Principal of Branch Normal College, Pine Bluff, Arkansas

**Sept. 27, 1875**—Opened Branch Normal College in Pine Bluff with seven students

## Jim Crow Era *1877-1964*

**Jan. 30, 1882**—Relocated Branch Normal College to the western edge of Pine Bluff

**1889**—Second M.A., Ohio University

**1898**—Co-founded Arkansas Teachers Association with fellow educator R. C. Childress.

**1898 to 1904**—First President, Arkansas Teachers Association

**1901–1902**—Last School Years as Principal at Branch Normal College

**1904–1910**—Principal at Merrill High School in Pine Bluff

**Jan. 11, 1911**—Died in Pine Bluff

**Jan. 14, 1911**—Buried at Waldheim Cemetery, Forest Park, Illinois

## CHAPTER 15

# Timeline: Branch Normal College

1873—Arkansas Act No. 97 established Branch Normal College.

Aug. 18, 1875—Joseph Carter Corbin hired by the Arkansas Industrial University Board of Trustees as principal.

Sept. 27, 1875—Professor Corbin opened Branch Normal College with seven students.

June 10, 1880—University Board of Trustees appropriated $3,000 of state funds to purchase ten acres of land for a new school site and building, near corporate limits of the city of Pine Bluff. The Branch Normal Committee, consisting of the University Trustees, Governor William R. Miller, William E. Thompson, and Grandison D. Royston, were directed to select the land and contract for the building. The committee went to Pine Bluff and purchased twenty acres of woodland for $700.00.[1]

June 7, 1881—Professor Corbin was permitted to omit Geometry, Differential and Integral Calculus, and Logic from the Normal Course.[2]

Jan. 30, 1882—Professor Corbin relocated Branch Normal College to a twenty-acre site on the western edge of city of Pine Bluff.[3]

1882—James Carter Smith was awarded the first bachelor's degree. He was the first graduate hired as a teacher at Branch Normal College, June 6, 1882, at a salary of forty dollars a month.[4]

June 9, 1882—Branch Normal Committee (Report to the Board): "the Committee appointed by you at your annual meeting in June 1880 to contract for and superintend the erection of a Building for Branch Normal College at or near the incorporated limits of the city of Pine Bluff in the County of Jefferson...discharging the duty assigned...did contract with the firm of Harding & Bailey...of Little Rock...to build a two story brick house...with four rooms in lower story and a hall in the upper story. Rooms in the lower story were twelve feet high. The hall in the upper story was 40 by 60 feet by sixteen feet high. The building cost was nine thousand, nine hundred and thirty dollars. Said college is now occupied and used as such...by Professor J. C. Corbin."[5]

June 13, 1882—Resolution by Trustee W. E. Thompson and adopted by Board of Trustees, authorized Branch Normal Committee to erect two cottage houses at a cost not to exceed eight hundred dollars each. One cottage was to be used by the principal as a residence; the other cottage was to be used as a boarding house for the benefit of students. The buildings were to be rented by the Committee to the principal and some competent and reliable person on the recommendation of the principal at a reasonable rate. The boarding house was to be under the control and management of the principal.[6]

1883—Alice A. Childress became the first female graduate of Branch Normal College.

**June 9, 1883**—Branch Normal Committee authorized and instructed Professor Corbin to collect from all non-beneficiary students one dollar per month for tuition. Additional teachers were to be hired from this sum, not to exceed a salary of $30 per month.

**June 9, 1883**—A modified course of study was adopted as recommended by Professor Corbin. Students who completed the modified course of study were entitled to a certificate of scholarship. Those who completed the course as published in the Report of the Arkansas Industrial University were entitled to the Normal Diploma.[7]

**June 14, 1884**—University Board of Trustees authorized publication of five hundred catalogues and a circular by Professor J. C. Corbin.[8]

1886—The first Licentiate of Instruction (LI) degree was awarded.

1887—The Girls Dormitory was erected. It was the first dormitory authorized by the University Board of Trustees.

1889—University Board of Trustees authorized $1,000 to furnish the Girls Dormitory.[9]

1890—The Legislature of 1890-91 appropriated $5,000 to build shops for Branch Normal College.[10]

1891—Branch Normal College became a land-grant institution.

**Nov. 30, 1892**—The Branch Normal Committee requested Professor C. V. Kerr to draw up plans and specifications for the shop buildings. The contract was awarded to W. S. Helton for $3,022 for a brick building measuring 70 feet by 70 feet with four shop rooms, a boiler room, a coal bin, and a court. The committee hired Mr. George P. Eustace, who had previously worked for the Arkansas Industrial University, at a salary of $1,000 per year. Eustace remained in charge of the shops until July 1892 when W. S. Harris of Virginia was hired as a replacement at a salary of $1,200 per annum.[11]

**June 6, 1893**—A resolution by Trustee Langford and adopted by the board instructed the principal and faculty to establish the demerit system as practiced at the Arkansas Industrial University. The Branch Normal College professors were to organize themselves into a faculty with a chairman and secretary. Faculty was to make reports to the Board of Trustees. Professors in the shops were to be considered members of the faculty. Professor W. S. Harris's salary increased to fourteen hundred dollars and he was to assume all instruction in machine and wood shops classes. The salary of A. E. Smith (Assistant Superintendent of Shops) was increased to $900 per annum with the requirement to provide all instruction in blacksmith and foundry shops. Professor Harris was directed to collect all matriculation and tuition fees and all other monies, and transmit to the Secretary of the Board of Trustees at Fayetteville. Professor Harris was to keep a correct record of all students entering Branch Normal College and keep a record of the demerit system for inspection by the Board of Trustees and faculty.[12]

**June 6, 1893**—Pine Bluff. Board of Trustees Election of Principal, Teachers & Salaries.
J. C. Corbin, Principal, $1,600.00.
J. C. Smith, Assistant, $700.
T. G. Childress, Assistant, $600.
W. S. Harris, Superintendent of Shops, $1,400.
A. E. Smith, Assistant Superintendent of Shops, $900.[13]

**1893**—A joint Arkansas House and Senate Committee was appointed to visit and investigate Branch Normal College.

*The Majority Committee Report Findings:*
"The Branch Normal College is suitably located and ought to be made to promote the interests for which it was founded, but your committee is of the opinion, in fact, would recommend that it be maintained on an improved and better basis than the one which it is now conducted. We believe it essential to maintain this school. From observation and investigation, your committee is of the opinion that the best interest of this school demands a change in management, or Principal.

"Professor Corbin stands fair among the people of Pine Bluff, and is considered a good and moral man, with a finished education, but in view of the fact he has been so long connected with the institution, and his failure or neglect to give more attention to the normal features of the school and his carelessness in business methods, a change should be made. Therefore Your committee recommend that he be displaced and some well qualified Educator of his race, a man of good executive ability, and a man who understands and appreciates the normal features of the institution be secured."

*The Minority Report by J. P. H. Russ, who dissented from the majority vote but agreed with the majority findings regarding the normal feature being ignored:*
"The black man is profoundly interested in the education of his children, but dwells in heat and cold and sun and storm with his wife and children, does not wish to be taxed in order that a favored few may have collegiate advantages allowed to their children, therefore solely in interest of ninety-nine percent of the colored people of Arkansas, I ask that the Branch Normal at Pine Bluff be abolished, that the property and fixtures be sold, that the proceeds be turned over to the common school fund for the benefit of the colored people, in order to educate the masses to the extent of a good common school education. The colored people of the state have abundant College facilities for which they are paying without having the poor to give collegiate education to the more favored of the race."[14]

Oct. 30, 1893—Miss Anna Petillo began her duties as teacher in the Literary Department.

June 17, 1897—Fayetteville. Board of Trustees Election of Principal, Teachers &, Salaries.
On motion of Trustee Yates, $2,800 appropriated by the Legislature for Professor Corbin (Principal) was increased to $3,200 so that his salary would remain at $1,600 annually.

The extra $400 was to be paid out of the Branch Normal Morrill fund.

J. C. Smith, $900.

T. G. Childress, $700.

Professor Annie G. Freeman, $600.

W. S. Harris, Assistant Superintendent, Mechanical Department (salary not listed).

A. E. Smith, Machine & Blacksmith Shops (salary not listed). Lorenzo Ellis, Engineer[15] (salary not listed).

**July 29, 1897**—Little Rock. Board of Trustees Meeting.

On Motion of Trustee Langford, W. S. Harris elected Treasurer of Branch Normal College for the year ending June 30, 1898, at a salary of $100 per annum with a performance bond requirement of $50,000.

The performance bond was delivered the same date to the Governor to be filed with the Secretary of State. $30,000 of the surety bond was guaranteed by Trustee Langford; H. A. McCoy—$2,000; Lerris Roth—$5,000; H. C. Fox—$5,000; Wiley Jones—$5,000; and Arthur Murray—$5,000.

On motion of Trustee Langford, Louise Corbin was elected Fourth Assistant Teacher for Sewing and Industrial Teacher for females, at a salary of $300.

On motion of Trustee Cook and Langford, Professor Corbin was authorized to purchase an organ, sewing machines, and heating apparatus for Branch Normal College.[16]

**Dec. 30, 1897**—E. K. Braley elected Assistant Superintendent of Machine and Blacksmith Shops to serve until June 30, 1898, to fill the unexpired term of A. E. Smith.[17]

**June 14, 1898**—Fayetteville. Board of Trustees Election of Principal, Teachers & Salaries.

J. C. Corbin, Principal and Professor of Mathematics, $1600.

J. C. Smith, First Assistant, $900.

T. G. Childress, Second Assistant, $600.

Annie C. Freeman, Third Assistant, $600.

Louisa M. Corbin, Fourth Assistant, $300.

W. S. Harris, Assistant Superintendent of Mechanical Department and Treasurer, $1,500.

A. E. Smith, Instructor Machine and Blacksmith Shops, $900.

Lorenzo Ellis, Engineer, $420.[18]

**June 15, 1898**—Fayetteville. C. E. Houghton of Ithaca, New York, elected Superintendent of Mechanic Arts and Professor of Mechanical Engineering for the University and Branch Normal for the year ending June 30, 1899, at a salary of $2,000.[19]

**June 13, 1899**—Board of Trustees Election of Principal, Teachers & Salaries.

J. C. Corbin, Principal and Professor of Mathematics, $1,600.

J. C. Smith First Assistant $900.

T. G. Childress, Second Assistant, $600.

Annie C. Freeman, Third Assistant, $600.

Louisa M. Corbin, Fourth Assistant, $300.

W. S. Harris, Assistant Superintendent, Mechanical Department, $1,600.

E. K. Braley, Instructor, Machine and Blacksmith Shops $900.

Lorenzo Ellis, Engineer, $420.[20]

**June 15, 1899**—Fayetteville

On motion of Trustee McDonough, W. H. Langford was elected agent to represent the University Board at Branch Normal

College. W. S. Harris was permitted to purchase such machinery as needed and to make other necessary improvements to campus subject to the advice, consent, and approval of said agent (Trustee Langford). On motion of Trustee T. A. Futrell, W. S. Harris was elected Treasurer of Branch Normal College.[21]

**August 7, 1899**—Little Rock

On motion of Trustee V. Y. Cook, E. K. Braley's salary was increased to $1,000. Lorenzo Ellis's salary to $480.[22]

**Nov. 4, 1899**—Pine Bluff. Special Session of the Board of Trustees. The Board spent several hours in thorough examination of the college buildings, work shops, machinery and grounds conferring with the principal and his assistants in relation to the condition of the institution and its wants and needs.

Professor J. C. Corbin was authorized to purchase two writing machines and three sewing machines with a specified limit from the Morrill Fund, and furnishing for the dormitory from the Contingent and Incidental Funds—all subject to the consent and approval of the Agent and Treasurer of Branch Normal College.

On motion of Trustee Cook, salary of J. C. Corbin increased to $1,800, James C. Smith to $1,000, Thomas Childress to $1,000, Louisa M. Corbin to $600. Treasurer of the college instructed to hereafter pay all of said salaries, including Annie C. Freeman, from the Morrill Fund belonging to the institution.

On motion of Trustee Seawell, the Treasurer of Branch Normal authorized to pay the salary of the President of the University out of the Branch Normal College Morrill Fund, without violating the Act of Congress, creating the Fund.

126

On motion of Trustee Seawell, all claims paid from the Branch Normal College Funds, excepting employees located at Fayetteville, shall be approved by the Agent-Trustee Langford and Treasurer of said institutions.

On recommendation of the Governor, the purchase of a Nash Gasoline Engine for Branch Normal College was left to the Superintendent of the Mechanical Arts and Agent Langford, with instructions to pay out of the Morrill Fund.[23]

**June 19, 1900**—Fayetteville
On motion of Trustee Seawell, the Superintendent of Mechanic Arts was permitted to remove the Nash Gas Engine from Branch Normal College to the University at Fayetteville, the expense paid by the University.[24]

**June 25, 1900**—Little Rock. Board of Trustees Election of Principal, Teachers & Salaries.
For the year ending June 30, 1901
J. C. Corbin, Principal and Professor of Mathematics, $1,800.
J. C. Smith, First Assistant, $1,200.
T. G. Childress, Second Assistant, $1,000.
Annie C. Freeman, Third Assistant, $750.
Louisa M. Corbin, Fourth Assistant, $600.
C. E. Houghton, Superintendent of the Mechanical Department, $1,800.
E. K. Braley, Instructor of Machines and Blacksmith, $1,200.
Lorenzo Ellis, Engineer, $480.[25]

**June 19, 1901**—Fayetteville. Board of Trustees Election of Principal, Teacher & Salaries.
For the year ending June 20, 1902
On motion of Trustee Cook the following Teachers and

Instructors were elected to serve Branch Normal College and their salaries:

J. C. Smith, First Assistant, $1,200.

T. G. Childress, Second Assistant, $1,000.

Annie C. Freeman, Third Assistant, $750.

Louisa M. Corbin, Fourth Assistant, $600.

C. E. Houghton, Superintendent of Mechanical Arts Department, $1,800.

W. S. Harris, Assistant Superintendent of Mechanical Arts Department, $1,800.

E. K. Braley, Instructor Machine and Blacksmith Shops, $1,200.

Lorenzo Ellis, Engineer, $480.

On motion of Trustee Mitchell, J. C. Corbin elected Principal of Branch Normal College at salary of $1,800 per annum.[26]

June 11, 1902—Pine Bluff. W. H. Langford, President of Citizens' Bank, certify that W. S. Harris, Treasurer of Branch Normal College, has on deposit in this bank, $8,337.22.[27]

June 17, 1902—Board of Trustees Meeting, Fayetteville. "The selection of teachers for the Branch Normal College is referred to the Branch Normal Committee" by the Board of Trustees.[28]

June 19, 1902—Professor Corbin's tenure at Branch Normal College came to an end. Isaac Fisher, a young educator from the Tuskegee Institute, succeeded Professor Corbin. Losing his appeal for reinstatement, Professor Corbin became principal of Merrill High School in Pine Bluff.

# Author's Notes

William J. Simmons's *Men of Mark* provided the most authoritative and comprehensive biography of Joseph Carter Corbin. All Corbin researchers have referred to *Men of Mark*.

The United States Census and city street directories were basic to establishing the family timeline and chronology of Corbin's life.

A lack of records hindered accumulating information about Corbin's sisters, his affiliation with churches in Little Rock and Pine Bluff, the institution where his doctoral degree was awarded, and other matters of interest.

Neither African American newspapers nor white newspapers proved to be significant primary sources on Professor Corbin.

The residence and activities of Joseph Carter Corbin between 1853 and 1860 remain of interest. The author was unable to document residence and teaching in Louisville, Kentucky, during this timeframe, as stated in *Men of Mark*.

Regarding the question of whether Professor Corbin and Mrs. Corbin had five children or six, this researcher and her associates were able to document five children. We note that Louisa M. Corbin quoted five children in Corbin's obituary in the *Mathematical Monthly*. Vital statistics records were unavailable in Cincinnati. A child, Joseph Corbin, age eleven months, died April 13, 1867, in Cincinnati, but his parentage could not be established. The Hamilton County Court House in Cincinnati suffered four fires prior to 1884, and stated this: "As the result of the four separate fires, the records prior to 1884 have been reconstructed but are not all intact and the fires probably account for their absences."

We did not find the Dental School that John Ward Corbin attended but ruled out Meharry Dental School, Howard University Dental School, and Northwestern University Dental School.

The John Quincy Adams Papers, 1856–1935, at the Minnesota Historical Society Library did not document Adams's role in Arkansas Republican politics during Reconstruction, or his role as "Assistant Superintendent of Public Instruction to his uncle, Joseph Carter Corbin."

Professor Corbin's Annual Reports to the Board of Trustees of the University of Arkansas were the most useful primary sources in understanding the challenges, successes, and setbacks at Branch Normal College, as well as the University's Board of Trustees Minutes.

James P. Brawley noted that "there seems to be a belief among many white people that Negro schools do not need as much money as white schools...and that Negro administrators and educators cannot use or administer large sums of money." White administrative and monetary control over Branch Normal College is well documented when Trustee Langford became "Agent of the Board" and was successful in getting Professor William S. Harris elected Treasurer of Branch Normal College. Hostilities toward liberal arts and teacher education for African Americans may also have been factors in whites taking control of the school, as well as paternalism and racism.

Unlike the situation with historically black colleges—which were founded by the Freedmen's Aid Society and had individual, family, or foundation philanthropy to save the institutions or set them on a new course of financial survival—it was the Morrill Act of 1890 that was of great financial benefit to Branch Normal College and Arkansas Industrial University.

The Corbin family was a remarkable family by any standard. They lifted themselves up through education, which enabled them to lift up others. Dr. Martin Luther King Jr. said, "All labor that uplifts humanity has dignity and importance and should be undertaken with painstaking excellence." Professor Corbin carried out his duties at Branch Normal College with "painstaking excellence," and no one did more to encourage the evolution of Branch Normal College.

According to the *Appeal*, January 14, 1911, the Corbin family "was a Christian family of the Baptist persuasion, and the husbands of Margaret, Belle, Susan, and Mary were Baptist preachers. All were teachers at some period of their lives. Several were clever vocalists, and musicians."

The freed men and women had suffered the degrading aspects of slavery. They were illiterate, having been denied the opportunity for education. They were considered inferior, incapable of learning or becoming educated. We are thankful for educators like Professor Corbin, whose courage, vision, dedication, and perseverance shaped institutions of learning and students' aspiration for education at a critical time following emancipation from slavery. As founder, first professor, and administrator of Branch Normal College, his leadership went beyond education. It was manifested in the secular and social affairs of Pine Bluff.

Branch Normal College is unique among historically black colleges. It began as a branch of a major southern white university, the University of Arkansas in Fayetteville. No other black college is known to have had this pattern of development. Its original mission was to train teachers; the agricultural studies were not a part of this college's purpose until the change of name in 1921 to Agricultural, Mechanical, and Normal College.

Branch Normal College (AM&N, UAPB) is unique because its founder was an African American. Branch Normal College produced teachers for the emerging Negro Normal Schools of Arkansas, under Professor Corbin. The first Bachelor of Arts degree (1882) and the Licentiate of Instruction degree (1886) were awarded under Professor Corbin. By 1896, Professor James C. Smith and Professor Thomas Childress (graduates of Branch Normal College) were providing trained leadership for the Negro Normal Schools' Teachers' Institutes along with Professor Corbin.

Branch Normal College repudiated the "propaganda of history" that nothing good came out of Reconstruction. In *Black Reconstruction in America*, W. E. B. Du Bois stated that the "advance of the Negro in education," and especially the "preparing of his own teachers," crown the accomplishments of Reconstruction. "Had it not been for these 'carpetbaggers' who deserve to be remembered and honored, for the development of black schools, and colleges, the Negro would to all intents and purposes, have been driven back to slavery."[1] Poor whites and African Americans alike benefited from the creation of public schools.

Branch Normal College repudiated the claim that African Americans were inferior and incapable of learning or becoming educated. Branch Normal College graduates were successful. Five graduates of AM&N have given presidential leadership to the school: Dr. Lawrence A. Davis Sr., Dr. Charles Walker, Dr. Carolyn Blakely, Dr. Lawrence A. Davis Jr., and Dr. Calvin Johnson.

John William Graves in his analysis of Reconstruction in Arkansas, *Town and Country: Race Relations and Urban Development in Arkansas, 1865-1905*, made the following astute statement:

> The terms "black reconstruction," "Negro domination," or "Negro rule" are misnomers, or at the most half-truth as applied to Arkansas as the Black population barely accounted for more than a fourth of the state population. No Negro served as governor or lieutenant governor or sat on the Supreme Court, or was elected to Congress from Arkansas under the Reconstruction administration. Blacks knew perfectly well that they were often regarded by whites as inherently unfit for self-government and tended to thrust their best men forward, especially for the higher and more important offices. Such black spokesmen as Joseph Carter Corbin and Mifflin W. Gibbs, Municipal Judge of Little Rock, and others were able to command considerable respect from both races.[2]

A lecture by Principal Isaac Fisher on what the state has a right to expect from persons trained at Branch Normal College and the University of Arkansas cited these expectations: to perpetuate knowledge and the rational rule of reason, to promote the social order and economic growth, and to reconcile every wrong that exists in the body politic. These expectations should remain today. I am sure that many of the graduates and leaders of the University of Arkansas at Pine Bluff have been guided or inspired by the philosophy of Professor John Brown Watson, president of AM&N College from 1928 to 1942, who said:

> The end of education is to know God and the laws and purposes of his universe, and to reconcile one's life with these laws. The first aim of a good college is not to teach books but the meaning and purpose of life. Hard study and the learning of books are only a means to this end. We develop Power, Courage, Determination and go out to achieve Truth, Wisdom and Justice. If we do not come to this, the cost of schooling is wasted.

Gladys Turner Finney
2017

# A Timeline of Reconstruction, 1865–1877

Reconstruction is the time following the Civil War when the United States attempted to reunite and heal the nation.

**1865**
Congress creates the Freedmen's Bureau, March 8, 1865, to aid the emancipated slaves.

End of the Civil War, April 9, 1865. Confederate General Robert E. Lee surrenders to Union General Ulysses S. Grant at Appomattox.

President Abraham Lincoln is assassinated, April 15, 1865. Vice President Andrew Johnson becomes president.

President Andrew Johnson presents plans for Reconstruction.

Thirteenth Amendment to the U.S. Constitution, ratified December 6, 1865, abolishes slavery in the United States.

## 1866

Reconstruction Acts are passed by Congress over President Johnson's veto. President Johnson does not favor equality for the former slaves.

Republican Party Convention Platform, July 30, 1866, in New Orleans includes equality for African Americans.

## 1868

Fourteenth Amendment to the Constitution, ratified July 9, 1865, grants citizenship to former slaves and their descendants, and guarantees equal protection under the laws of the United States.

Francis L. Cardozo, an African American, is elected secretary of state in South Carolina (1868–1872). He is the first African American to hold statewide office in the United States.

Oscar J. Dunn, ex-slave, is inaugurated (June 13, 1868) as lieutenant governor of Louisiana. He dies in office (November 22, 1871) and is succeeded by P. B. S. Pinchback.

P. B. S. Pinchback of New Orleans is elected Louisiana state senator.

John Willis Menard is elected to the U.S. Congress from Louisiana. He is denied admission due to election challenges over disputed election returns. Neither he nor his opponent is seated. When allowed to plead his case before the Congress (February 27, 1869) John W. Menard becomes the first African American to speak on the floor of the U.S. House of Representatives.

General Ulysses S. Grant (Republican) is elected president of the United States, November 2, 1868.

The Freedmen's Bureau is abolished in December 1868.

## 1870

Joseph H. Rainey of South Carolina is the first African American sworn in as a member of the U.S. House of Representatives, December 12, 1870.

Fifteenth Amendment to the Constitution is ratified on March 30, 1870, granting African American males the right to vote.

Jonathan Jasper Wright is elected February 1, 1870, to the South Carolina Supreme Court.

## 1872

Lieutenant Governor P. B. S. Pinchback serves as governor of Louisiana, December 9, 1872, to January 13, 1873. He is the first African American to serve as governor of a state. Henry A. Corbin (Joseph Carter Corbin's brother) serves as Pinchback's personal secretary.

The Freedmen's Bank closes after African American depositors lose more than a million dollars in deposits.

## 1875

Congress enacts the Civil Rights Act of 1875 on March 1, guaranteeing equal treatment to African Americans in public accommodations, transportation, and jury duty. The act is later declared unconstitutional on October 15, 1883, by the Supreme Court.

## 1876

44th Congress. United States Senate votes, March 8, 1876, not to seat Senator-Elect P. B. S. Pinchback as U.S. senator from Louisiana, stemming out of election challenges in the 1872 election. Democrats now control Congress and uphold election of his opponent.

## 1877

In events surrounding the Hayes-Tilden Presidential Election Compromise, Samuel Tilden, Democratic presidential candidate, wins the popular vote. Southern Democratic leaders of the House of Representatives agree to award Rutherford B. Hayes (Republican) the disputed electoral votes of Florida and South Carolina in exchange for the withdrawal of the last federal troops from the South. Congress votes to accept the recommendation of the Election Commission to end the election impasse of 1876. Black Republicans feel betrayed. The political power shifts back to southern states' previous slave owners, and to Democratic legislatures in the South, effectively ending the Reconstruction Era.

Rutherford B. Hayes is inaugurated, March 5, 1877, as president of the United States.

President Hayes withdraws the last federal troops from South Carolina, ending the federal government's presence—also ending the protection of rights of African Americans in the South.

Robert Brown Elliott, who was elected attorney general of South Carolina in 1876, yields office of attorney general.

# African Americans in the United States Congress during the Reconstruction Era

## 1869–1871

41st Congress. There were three African American members in the U.S. House of Representatives: Joseph H. Rainey of South Carolina, Representative Robert Brown Elliott from the 3rd District of South Carolina, and Jefferson F. Long of Georgia. Hiram Revels (Republican) from Mississippi is the first black senator.

## 1871–1873

42nd Congress. Five African Americans serve in the 42nd Congress of the United States: Joseph H. Rainey, Robert Carlos De Large, and Robert Brown Elliott of South Carolina; Benjamin T. Turner of Alabama; and Josiah T. Walls of Florida.

## 1873–1875

43rd Congress. Six African Americans serve in the 43rd Congress of the United States, House of Representatives:

Richard Cain, South Carolina
Robert Brown Elliott, South Carolina
John R. Lynch, Mississippi
Alonzo J. Ransier, South Carolina
Joseph H. Rainey, South Carolina
Josiah T. Walls, Florida

## 1875–1877

44th Congress. African Americans to serve in the 44th Congress of the United States:

Blanche K. Bruce, Senator, Mississippi

Jeremiah Haralson, Alabama
John A. Hyman, North Carolina
John R. Lynch, Mississippi
Charles E. Nash, Louisiana
Joseph H. Rainey, South Carolina
James T. Rapier, Alabama
Robert Smalls, South Carolina
Josiah T. Walls, Florida

## 1877–1879

45th Congress. African Americans to serve in the 45th Congress of the United States:

Blanche K. Bruce, Mississippi, U.S. Senate

Richard H. Cain, South Carolina
John R. Lynch, Mississippi
Joseph H. Rainey, South Carolina
Robert Smalls, South Carolina

## Superintendents of Education during the Reconstruction Era

| *Arkansas* | Joseph Carter Corbin | 1872–1874 |
| *Florida* | Jonathan Gibbs | 1873–1875 |
| *Louisiana* | William G. Brown | 1873–1877 |
| *Mississippi* | Thomas W. Cardoz | 1874–1876 |

# Corbin Family Register

## Generation I

### 1. WILLIAM CORBIN.

He was born Abt. 1798 in Virginia, USA. He died on 29 Jan 1875 in Cincinnati, Hamilton, Ohio, USA [1, 2, 3]. Burial in Cincinnati, Hamilton, Ohio, USA.

Notes for William Corbin:
General Notes: 1870 Cincinnati City Directory, Wm. h. 141 Smith Street.

### SUSAN MORDECAI CARTER.

She was born Abt. 1804 in Virginia, USA. She died on 09 Feb 1874 in Cincinnati, Hamilton, Ohio, USA [4, 5]. Burial in Cincinnati, Hamilton, Ohio, USA.

Notes for Susan Mordecai Carter:
General Notes: Mrs. Susan M. Corbin (mother of Hon. J. C. Corbin, superintendent of public instruction (death) at her late residence, 141 Smith Street, Cincinnati, Ohio, on Sunday evening, 8th instant.)

*Of the sainted dead we may justly say—*
"Servant of God, well done,
Rest from thy blest employ:

The battle's fought, the victory won—
Enter thy Master's joy."
*Morning Republican*, Little Rock, Arkansas, 2-10-1874.

## WILLIAM CORBIN & SUSAN MORDECAI CARTER.

They were married on 23 Jan 1825 in Chillicothe, Ross, Ohio, USA
[6]. They had 11 children.

## Children:

**2. i. MARGARET PRISCILLA CORBIN.**
She was born Abt. 1824 in Ohio, USA.

**3. ii. SUSAN CORBIN.**
She was born Abt. 1829 in Chillicothe, Ross, Ohio, USA.

**iii. ELIZABETH CORBIN.**
She was born Abt. 1830 in Chillicothe, Ross, Ohio, USA. She
died on 14 Aug 1893 in Cincinnati, Hamilton, Ohio, USA [7].
Burial in Cincinnati, Hamilton, Ohio, USA [8].

**iv. ISABELLA CORBIN.**
She was born Abt. 1833.

**4. v. JOSEPH CARTER CORBIN.**
He was born on 26 Mar 1833 in Chillicothe, Ross, Ohio, USA.
He married Mary Jane Ward. They were married on 16 Sep
1866 in Cincinnati, Hamilton, Ohio, USA [6]. He died on 11
Jan 1911 in Pine Bluff, Jefferson, Arkansas, USA. Burial on 14
Jan 1911 in Forest Park, Cook, Illinois, USA [9, 10, 11].
J. C. Corbin was a member of the Board of Trustees of St. Paul
Missionary Baptist Church, Pine Bluff [28].

**vi. WILLIAM B. CORBIN.**
He was born Abt. 1835.

**vii. LUCY CORBIN.**
She was born Abt. 1838 [12, 13].

**5. viii. JOHN H. CORBIN.**
He was born Abt. 1842 in Ohio, USA. He married Virginia C.
Baker. They were married on 08 Feb 1871 in Cincinnati,
Hamilton, Ohio, USA [14].
He died on 19 Sep 1878 in New Orleans, Orleans, Louisiana,
USA [15].

### ix. MARGARET A. CORBIN.

She was born Abt. 1842.

### x. MARY CORBIN.

She was born Abt. 1843.

### xi. HENRY A. CORBIN.

He was born Abt. 1845. He died on 05 Sep 1878 in New Orleans, Orleans, Louisiana, USA [16]. Burial in Cincinnati, Hamilton, Ohio, USA.

Notes for Henry A. Corbin:

General Notes: Henry A. Corbin ranked among the "socially prominent" in New Orleans by the "number of positions of trust and honor" held during Reconstruction.

Henry A. Corbin, a graduate of an Ohio college, edited P. B. S. Pinchback's *Weekly Louisianian*, 1872 to 1874. He was later secretary of the board of education and a state tax collector.

John W. Blassingame, *Black New Orleans 1860-1880*. University of Chicago Press, 1973, pp. 132, 157.

Henry A. Corbin was P. B. S. Pinchback's secretary while he was Lieutenant Governor (1872). In 1871, Pinchback borrowed $40,000 from Henry A. Corbin to contribute to the purchase of a large section of vacant land to become a city park.

Henry A. Corbin traveled with Pinchback during his infamous visit to the Republican National Committee Headquarters in 1872.

James Haskins, *The First Black Governor, Pin[c]kney Benton Stewart Pinchback*. Trenton, NJ: Africa World Press, 1996, p. 86.

The New Orleans City Directory of 1878 lists Henry A. Corbin as the tax collector of the 6th District until the time of his death.

James M. Trotter's book *Music* and some highly musical people note that Henry A. Corbin was an accomplished violinist who learned the violin under a German teacher and under Professor Bonnivard.

# Generation II

**2. MARGARET PRISCILLA CORBIN-2** (William Corbin-1).
She was born Abt. 1824 in Ohio, USA.
**HENRY ADAMS.**
He was born on 17 Dec 1802 in Franklin, Georgia, USA [17]. He
died on 03 Nov 1872.
   Notes for Henry Adams:
   General Notes: Pastor of Fifth Street Baptist Church,
Louisville, Kentucky, 1829-
      "Through his instrumentality the General Association of
      Colored Baptists was organized August 3, 1869, in the first
      Baptist church in Lexington. He was elected moderator."
      "To him is largely due the credit for establishing
      Kentucky State University."
      William J. Simmons, "Rev. Henry Adams, A Faithful
      Pastor—A Good Man," in *Men of Mark*, pp. 798–800.

**HENRY ADAMS & MARGARET PRISCILLA CORBIN.**
They had 5 children.

## Children:

   **i. SUSAN E. ADAMS.**
   **ii. MARGARET A. ADAMS.**
   **iii. JOHN QUINCY ADAMS.**
   He was born on 04 May 1846 in Louisville, Jefferson,
   Kentucky, USA [18]. He married Ella Bell Smith. They were
   married on 04 May 1892 in St Paul, Ramsey, Minnesota, USA
   [18]. He died on 04 Sep 1922 in St Paul, Ramsey, Minnesota,
   USA [18]. Burial in St Paul, Ramsey, Minnesota, USA.
   **iv. CYRUS FIELD ADAMS.**
   Birth date: July 18, 1858, Louisville, Kentucky. Death Date:
   February 18, 1942 Manitoba, Canada. *Source: University of
   Kentucky Libraries, "Notable Kentucky African Americans
   Database."*
      Notes for Cyrus Field Adams:
      General Notes: Cyrus Field Adams was free born to

Margaret Priscilla (Corbin) Adams and Reverend Henry Adams in Louisville, Kentucky. He taught German to the African-American public school teachers in Louisville, and was professor of the German language at the State University in Louisville. He was Manager of *The Appeal*. (Chicago). He was appointed to the Republican National Advisory Committee by Senator Marcus A. Hanna of Ohio during the Presidential Election of 1900 to elect William McKinley. He was also appointed Assistant Register of the United States Treasury. He held "one of the largest collection of stamps in the United States, and was a linguist in several languages." Cyrus Field Adams and his brother John Quincy Adams were active in Republican politics. Cyrus Field Adams Papers, 1876–1928, Minnesota Historical Society, St. Paul, Minnesota.

   **v. LEYOUS ADAMS.**

**3. SUSAN CORBIN-2** (William Corbin-1).
She was born Abt. 1829 in Chillicothe, Ross, Ohio, USA.

**PAYTON SIMS.**

**PAYTON SIMS & SUSAN CORBIN.**
They had 1 child.

**Child:**

   **i. JOSEPH SIMS.**

**4. JOSEPH CARTER CORBIN-2** (William Corbin-1).
He was born on 26 Mar 1833 in Chillicothe, Ross, Ohio, USA. He died on 11 Jan 1911 in Pine Bluff, Jefferson, Arkansas, USA. Burial on 14 Jan 1911 in Forest Park, Cook, Illinois, USA [9, 10, 11].
   Notes for Joseph Carter Corbin:
   General Notes: Educator Extraordinaire, Scholar, Musician.
      Elected 1872 State of Arkansas Superintendent of Public Education.
      President Board of Trustees, Arkansas Industrial University (now University of Arkansas, Fayetteville).

Founder and President of University of Arkansas at Pine Bluff.

Leader in Public Education Movement in Arkansas. Co-founder of first black state teacher organization.

"One of Ohio University's most distinguished and scholarly graduate of the mid 19th Century."

Born to free African-American parents (1833) Chillicothe, Ohio.

Became one of the most educated men of his day, earning a BA from Ohio University (1853) and two master's degrees from Ohio University, 1856 and 1859.

## MARY JANE WARD.

She was born Abt. 1833 in Kentucky, USA. She died on 28 Mar 1910 in Chicago, Cook, Illinois, USA [19, 20]. Burial on 31 Mar 1910 in Forest Park, Cook, Illinois, USA [21].

Notes for Mary Jane Ward:

General Notes: Mary Jane was a dressmaker in Cincinnati, Ohio, and shared a shop with another dressmaker. Little is known about her life as Mrs. Corbin in Little Rock and Pine Bluff. One source stated she was an art teacher at Branch Normal College. She was most likely a volunteer. She was not listed on the paid staff of the college.

## JOSEPH CARTER CORBIN & MARY JANE WARD.

They were married on 16 Sep 1866 in Cincinnati, Hamilton, Ohio, USA [6]. They had 5 children.

## Children:

### i. JOHN WARD CORBIN.

He was born Abt. 1867 in Cincinnati, Hamilton, Ohio, USA. He died on 08 Dec 1907 in Pine Bluff, Jefferson, Arkansas, USA. Burial on 27 Dec 1909 in Forest Park, Cook, Illinois, USA [19, 9, 22].

Notes for John Ward Corbin:

General Notes: John Ward Corbin graduated from Branch Normal College in the Class of 1888 with an LI degree. 1888–1890, he was a student at Oberlin College

(Preparatory Department) according to Oberlin College Records and Archives.

Occupation: Dentist in Chicago according to 1900 U.S. Census, 1900 Chicago City Directory, and Branch Normal College Alumni Records. Office: 2842 Stats, home 2738 Princeton Ave.

### ii. WILLIAM H. CORBIN.

He was born Abt. 1869 in Cincinnati, Hamilton, Ohio, USA. He died on 06 Oct 1929 in Pine Bluff, Jefferson, Arkansas, USA [9, 23]. Burial on 10 Oct 1929 in Forest Park, Cook, Illinois, USA [19, 9, 24]. Notes for William H. Corbin: General Notes: 1900 Chicago City Directory. William H. Corbin, stenographer. Home: 2736 Princeton Ave.

### iii. FAUSTINA CORBIN.

She was born Abt. 1873 in Little Rock, Pulaski, Arkansas, USA. She died on 01 Aug 1884 in Little Rock, Pulaski, Arkansas, USA [25]. Burial on 20 Feb 1886 in Cincinnati, Hamilton, Ohio, USA.

Notes for Faustina Corbin:
General Notes: Faustina Corbin was reinterred February 20, 1886 (from Oakland Cemetery, Little Rock) to Union Baptist Cemetery, Cincinnati, Ohio. Hamilton County, Ohio Burial Records, Vol 9, Union Baptist African American Cemetery, Part 2, p. 8.

### iv. PEA CORBIN.

She was born Abt. 1875 in Arkansas, USA [26].
Notes for Pea Corbin:
General Notes: Pea Corbin is listed in the 1880 U.S. Census as Age 5; Birth year 1875; Residence: Little Rock, Pulaski County, Arkansas. Pea Corbin is presumed to have died young in Arkansas. No other records were found on her.

### v. LOUISA M. CORBIN.

She was born Abt. 1876 in Arkansas, USA.
Notes for Louisa M. Corbin:
General Notes: Louisa Corbin was a teacher of sewing and industrial education at Branch Normal College. She was elected by the Board of Trustees as the "fourth Teacher Assistant," July 29, 1897, and was the second female to teach at Branch Normal College.

Louisa Corbin was enumerated as Luesa Corbin, East St. Louis, Ward 3, St. Clair County, Illinois in the 1910 Census where she was a boarder in the household of Crestes Hood, with other public school teachers.

From "A Brief History of the Social and Art Club (Pine Bluff )": A group of civic-minded black women met December 13, 1911, in the home of Mrs. Estell Edwards, and organized the Social and Art Club. Miss Louise Corbin (Daughter of the illustrious Prof. J. C. Corbin) was elected treasurer. The Social and Art Club became affiliated with the Arkansas State Federation in 1912, and with the National Federation in 1913. The purpose of the club was "to improve the spiritual, educational and civic development of Negro Women."

1912 Little Rock, Arkansas City Directory: Louise Corbin, 3701 XV 16th., Teacher.

1923 Chicago Directory: Louisa M. Corbin clerk, Industrial Comm of Illinois, residence 4555 Champlain Ave.?

1930 Chicago Street Directory: Louisa M. Corbin, clerk, Industrial Comm of Illinois, residence 4555 Champlain Ave.?

## 5. JOHN H. CORBIN-2 (William Corbin-1).

He was born Abt. 1842 in Ohio, USA. He died on 19 Sep 1878 in New Orleans, Orleans, Louisiana, USA [15]. Notes for John H. Corbin:

General Notes: John H. Corbin was the principal of McDonough School No 5. In New Orleans. There were originally 35 McDonough Schools, so the number is important. His school was located in the historic West-bank Algiers Neighborhood of New Orleans.

McDonough No 5 School, designed by William Freret in the "cottage school" style, opened in 1875 on Verret Street between Franklin (now Opelousas) and Market (now Slidell) Streets as a grammar and primary school for African American boys and girls. By 1909, the school had been turned over to white students. The building was located on the site currently occupied by the Berhman School Gymnasium.

Both John H. Corbin and his brother Henry A. Corbin died from yellow fever in the Yellow Fever epidemic of 1878.

1875 Cincinnati Street Directory. John H. Corbin, Messenger at 65 w. 3rd. Street. residence 293 John St.

1873 Cincinnati Street Directory. John H. Corbin, clerk, home 293 John Street.

1870 Cincinnati City Directory. J. H. Corbin, porter, bds Smith Street.

October 16, 1861 to October 9, 1865 fought in the Civil War with the Wisconsin Volunteers Infantry, Company A. Promoted to Quartermaster Sergeant, August 31, 1862. Discharged October 9, 1865 at Mobile, Alabama.

## VIRGINIA C. BAKER.

Daughter of Anna Baker. She was born in Alabama, USA.

Notes for Virginia C. Baker:

General Notes:

1872 Cincinnati Street Directory. Jennie C. Corbin, Music Teacher. home. 293 John Street.

1875 Cincinnati Street Directory. Mrs. J. C. Corbin, Music Teacher. home. 293 John Street.

1880 Census: Residence, Springfield, Clark County, Ohio (widow). Living with mother, Anna Baker, and 5 year old son, Walter B. Corbin.

## JOHN H. CORBIN & VIRGINIA C. BAKER.

They were married on 08 Feb 1871 in Cincinnati, Hamilton, Ohio, USA [14]. They had 3 children.

## Children:

### i. OLFRED H. CORBIN.

He was born 1873 in Cincinnati, Hamilton, Ohio, USA [27]. He died on 12 Dec 1874 in Cincinnati, Hamilton, Ohio, USA [27]. Burial in Cincinnati, Hamilton, Ohio, USA [27].

Notes for Olfred H. Corbin:

General Notes: Address: 293 John Street, Cincinnati, Ohio. From Cincinnati Ohio Health Department Death Records: M . Col. S. Age at death 1 Year 12-12-1874. Marasmus; Dr. D. Newton. J. Epply (Funeral Home); Union Baptist (Burial).

**ii. JOHN CORBIN.**
He was born Jan 1875 in Cincinnati, Hamilton, Ohio, USA [27].
 Notes for John Corbin:
 General Notes: Address: 293 John Street, Cincinnati, Ohio.
**iii. WALTER B. CORBIN.**
He was born on 19 Jan 1875.

# Generation III

**6. JOHN QUINCY ADAMS-3** (Margaret Priscilla Corbin-2, William Corbin-1).
He was born on 04 May 1846 in Louisville, Jefferson, Kentucky, USA [18]. He died on 04 Sep 1922 in St Paul, Ramsey, Minnesota, USA [18]. Burial in St Paul, Ramsey, Minnesota, USA.
 Notes for John Quincy Adams:
 General Notes: John Quincy Adams was freeborn in Louisville, Kentucky, May 4, 1848, to Henry Adams and Margaret Priscilla (Corbin) Adams of Chillicothe, Ohio. He followed his uncle, Joseph Carter Corbin (1870-1876), to Little Rock, Arkansas, taught school there before taking a position as Assistant Superintendent of Public Instruction, twice served as Secretary of Arkansas Republican Convention. Also served as Engrossing Clerk for the (Arkansas) State Senate, and (Arkansas)Deputy Commissioner of Public Works.

John Q. Adams was privately educated at the elementary and secondary level in Fond du Lac, Wisconsin, Yellow Springs, Ohio, and graduated from Oberlin College. He was a newspaper publisher and editor, along with his brother, Cyrus Field Adams, of *The Appeal* which had offices in Minneapolis, Chicago, St. Louis, Dallas, and Washington, D.C.

John Quincy Adams, St. Paul Editor and Black Leader, David V. Taylor, p. 285.

John Quincy Adams (1848-1922), *The Black Past Remembered and Reclaimed*, p 3.

Special Dispatch on Meeting of Arkansas State Republican Convention (May 18, 1872) to *New York Times*, June 19, 1872: "The State Republican Convention met at noon today, to appoint delegates to Philadelphia and elect a new State

Central Committee. Judge Stephenson, of Helena was elected President; J. Q. Adams of Jefferson, Secretary."

## ELLA BELL SMITH.

## JOHN QUINCY ADAMS & ELLA BELL SMITH.
They were married on 04 May 1892 in St Paul, Ramsey, Minnesota, USA [18]. They had 4 children.

## Children:

### i. JOHN QUINCY ADAMS, JR.
He was born on 20 Jul 1896 in St Paul, Ramsey, Minnesota, USA.
### ii. ADINA ADAMS.
### iii. MARGARET ADAMS.
### iv. EDYTHELLA ADAMS.

## Sources:

1   *Cincinnati Daily Gazette*, 2/02/1875; 5.5.
2   *Daily Gazette* (Feb 10, 1874), Burial Permits Issued Feb 1, Giving Date of Death, Age and Nativity. Jan 29-Wm. F. Corbin -76 years- Virginia.
3   Cincinnati Birth and Death Records 1865-1912. William F. Corbin, MNM, Age 76; Address: 141 Smith St. Birth: Virginia; Cause of Death: Old Age; Physician: Dr. W. Carson; Undertaker: J. Epply; Burial: Union Baptist Cemetery.
4   *Daily Gazette* (Feb 10, 1874). Corbin-In this city, on the morning of the 9th. Mrs. Susan Mordecai Corbin, wife of Wm. Corbin, in the 72nd year of her age.
5   1866-1875 Cincinnati Birth and Death Records. Female, Colored, Married, 72 years. Death Date: February 9, 1874. Address: 141 Smith St. Birth: Virginia. Cause of death: Hepatitis; Physician: Dr. T. Bradford; Undertaker: J. Epply. Burial: Union Baptist Cemetery.
6   Jeffrey G. Herbert, Restored Hamilton County Ohio Marriages 1860-1869, Page 51, Code VB4. Sept. 16, 1866.

7   drc.libraries.uc.edu. FWS; Seamstress; Union Baptist Cemetery.

8   Ohio Deaths and Burial Index-1854-1897. Female White, Age
    60. Date of Death: August 14, 1893: Address Wehrman Ave.
    Birth: Ohio; Cause of Death: Sclerosis Cerebri; Physician: Dr. E.
    W. Mitchell; Undertaker: Porter; Burial: Union Baptist Cemetery.

9   Forest Home Cemetery. Residence: Pine Bluff, Arkansas, Int No.
    27387; Lot 44, Block F, Sub.c Date of Burial: December 27, 1909
    (from Oak Wood Cemetery). Cause of Death: Meningitis.
    Undertaker: F. J. Theorell.

10  Waldheim Cemetery Records. Residence: Pine Bluff, Ark.; Int.
    No. 38687; Lot 44, Block F, Sub. c. Remarks: 75 years.

11  Forest Home Cemetery Records. Residence/Place of Death: Pine
    Bluff, Arkansas. Int. No. 38687; Lot 44, Block F Sub C. Date of
    Burial: January 14, 1911; Cause of Death: Heart Failure;
    Physician: W. E. Williams; Undertaker: C. S. Jackson.

12  1850 U.S. Census

13  United States Census 1850, Entry for William Corbin.

14  Hamilton County Ohio Probate Court Records.

15  *Daily Picayune* (New Orleans), 1878-09-21, Pg. 2 col. 1. Death
    Date: 1878-09-19 Age: 36 years; Sex M.

16  *Daily Gazette* (Feb 10, 1874), 07 Sept. 1878. Corbin-In New
    Orleans, September 5, of yellow fever. Henry A. Corbin, son of
    the late William and Susan Corbin, in his 33rd year, formerly of
    this city.

17  Rev. William J. Simmons, *Men of Mark: Eminent, Progressive and
    Rising* (Cleveland, OH: Geo M. Rewell & Co., 1887/New York:
    Arno Press, 1968).

18  David V. Taylor, *Minnesota History*, Winter 1973, p. 285.

19  Certificate and Record of Death, Department of Health, City of
    Chicago.

20  Department of Health City of Chicago Certificate & Record of
    Death. Place of Birth: Kentucky; Date of Birth: 1833; Married;
    Age: 77; Occupation: Housewife from 1875 to 1910; Place of
    Death: 5738 Indiana Ave. - 2 years; Usual Residence: 6738
    Indiana Ave, Ward 30; Place of Burial: Waldheim Cemetery;
    Undertaker: Charles S. Jackson; Cause of Death: Dynamic Ileus;
    Informant: J. C. Corbin, 5738 Indiana Ave.

21  Waldheim Cemetery Records. Residence: 5138 Indiana Ave. Int.
    No. 37908; Lot 44, Block F, Sub. c 77 years.

22  Waldheim Cemetery Records. Residence: Pine Bluff, Ark. Int. No. 37397; Lot 44 F sub. c., 39 years.

23  Arkansas State Board of Health-Bureau of Vital Statistics Certificate of Death. Place of Death: Jefferson County, Vaugine Township, City of Pine Bluff. Male, Colored, Single, About 45, Retired Professor. Father: J. C. Corbin. Date of Death: October 6, 1929. Cause of Death: "Killed by crushing skull with some unknown implement by some unknown person." Operation preceded death (October 6, 1929): Crushed bone was removed; Inquest: Yes. Informant: James Jones, Jr. Place of Burial: Chicago, IL, October 8, 1929. Undertaker: Perry & Company.

24  Forest Home Cemetery Records. Residence/Place of Death: Pine Bluff, Arkansas, Int. No. 53199 Lot 44, Block F Sub C; Date of Burial: October 10, 1929. Remarks: 45 years. Cause of Death: Skull Fracture; Physician: J. H. Edwards; Undertaker: T. Edwin?

25  Little Rock Arkansas Register of Deaths, 1871-1881. Birth: Little Rock; Died: 8/1/1884; Last Place of Residence: Little Rock; How Long in state: Life; Place of death: Little Rock; Parents: J. C. and Mary J. Corbin; Cause of Death: Diphtheria; Medical Attendant: James C. Southall; Burial: Oakland.

26  1880 U.S. Census. Daughter to Head of Household.

27  Cincinnati Birth and Death Records 1865–1912.

28  St. Paul Missionary Baptist Church Cornerstone.

# Corbin Family Little Rock Residences

## 1871

Corbin, J. C., cld, reporter, Republican Office, bds 809 Izard. Little Rock City Directory, p. 51.

## 1872–1873

Corbin, J. C., assistant postmaster, post-office, res Ninth, bet Arch and Broadway. Little Rock City Directory, p. 63.

## 1877–1878

Corbin, J. C., teacher, rss 6th, 2d w of Victory. Little Rock Directory, p. 69.

## 1878

Corbin, Joseph C., c, teacher, rss 6th, 2d w of Victory. Little Rock Directory, p. 72.

## 1880

Corbin, Joseph C., c, teacher, 1408 W 6th Little Rock City Directory, p. 57.

**1881–1882**

Corbin, Prof. J. C., c, prin Normal College Pine Bluff, res 1407 w Sixth. Little Rock Directory, p. 61.

# College Catalogue

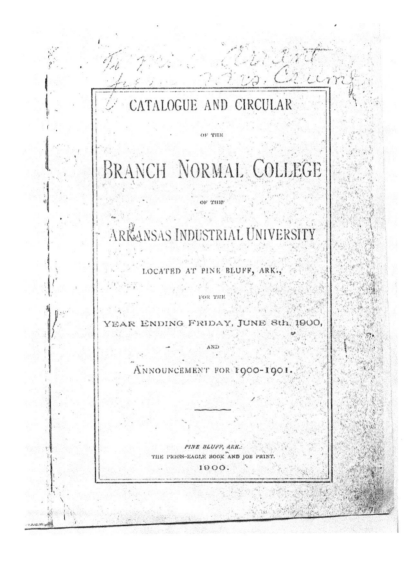

CATALOGUE AND CIRCULAR

OF THE

# BRANCH NORMAL COLLEGE

OF THE

## ARKANSAS INDUSTRIAL UNIVERSITY

LOCATED AT PINE BLUFF, ARK.,

FOR THE

YEAR ENDING FRIDAY, JUNE 8th, 1900,

AND

ANNOUNCEMENT FOR 1900-1901.

———

*PINE BLUFF, ARK.:*
THE PRESS-EAGLE BOOK AND JOB PRINT.
1900.

# ALUMNI ASSOCIATION.

The objects of this Association are to maintain the interest of the graduates in the institution and bring them into closer relation with the College. To this end all graduates are considered members. The Association holds meetings annually during commencement week. The officers of the Association for 1900 are :

REV. I. P. DANIELS, Little Rock.
MISS W. V. A. WATERHOUSE, Pine Bluff.

## LIST OF ALUMNI.

### 1882

1   James Carter Smith. A. B., professor, Branch Normal College.

### 1883.

2   *Alice A. Childress. A. B., professor, Branch Normal College.

### 1884.

3   John Gray Lucas, A. B., lawyer, Chicago, Ill.
4   Alexander L. Burnett, A. B., lawyer, Pine Bluff, Ark.
5   *Celis W George, A. B., minister, Texarkana, Ark.
6   *John P. Williams, A. B., teacher, Baxter, Ark.

### 1885. .

7   John C. Calhoun, A. B., teacher, Scott's, Ark.
8   Archibald B. Crump, A. B., principal. Texarkana, Ark.

### 1886

9   Jacob W Ricks, L. I., principal, Fordyce, Ark.
10   George W Bunn, L. I., M. D., Bonham, Texas.
11   Robert B. Williamson, L. I., M. D., Stamps, Ark.
12   *Richard S. Sanders, L. I., Chicago, Ill.
13   Nelson J. C. Johnson, L. I., Deputy County Clerk, Guthrie, Ok.
14   Isaiah P. Daniels, L. I., rector St. Phillip's Church, Little Rock, Ark.
15   Henry W Cook, L. I., M. D., Bonham, Texas.
16   Sterling P. Brown. L. I., principal, Edwards, Miss.

### 1888.

17   John W. Corbin, L. I., D. D. S., Chicago, Ill.
18   Lucinda Alexander, L. I., teacher, Pine Bluff. Ark.
19   Lawson T. Thomas, L. I., teacher, Lonoke, Ark.
20   J S. House, L. I., M. D., Sherrill, Ark.
21   Louis Bunn, L. I., teacher, Dry Run, Ark.
22   Wm. I. Pumphrey, L. I., teacher, Richmond, Ark.

## 1889.

23  J A. Andrews, L. I., teacher, Oklahoma.
24  W B. Cloman, L. I., principal, Dermott, Ark.
25  F. H. Howard, L. I., teacher, Camden, Ark.
26  George F. Pruitt, L. I., teacher, Phillips county, Ark.
27  *Benjamin E. Reed, L. I., barber, Pine Bluff, Ark.
28  Katie D. Wright, L. I., teacher, Cleveland county, Ark.
29  Thos. B. Childress, A. B., professor, Branch Normal College.
30  M. J Harrison, L. I., minister, Portland, Ark.
31  Anna C. Freeman, L. I., professor, Branch Normal College.

## 1890.

32  Elenora Davis, L. I., teacher, Pine Bluff, Ark.
33  David W. Briggs, L. I., teacher, Jefferson county, Ark.
34  Stephen W. Crump, L. I., principal, Pine Bluff, Ark.
35  *Emma McKay, L. I., teacher, Jefferson county, Ark.
36  Richard M. Allen, L. I., teacher, Hot Springs, Ark.
37  William H. Card, L. I., teacher, Covington, Ky.
38  John W Russell, L. I., teacher, Jefferson county, Ark.
39  William Waterhouse, L. I., teacher, Walnut Hill, Ark.
40  John M. Vealy, L. I., teacher, Mineral Springs, Ark.
41  Bennett J Brown, L. I., Magnolia, Ark.
42  Julian T. Chambliss, L. I., teacher, Greer, Ark.
43  Charles M. Critz, L. I., teacher, Bald Knob, Ark.

## 1891.

44  Adam Arrant, L. I., teacher, Camden, Ark.
45  Georgia House, L. I, teacher, Linwood, Ark.
46  Andrew Cobb, L. I., teacher, Parksdale, Ark.
47  Thaddeus Cobb, L. I., Chicago, Ill.
48  Zach. T Washington, L. I., teacher, Jefferson county, Ark.
49  R. B. Fagan, L. I., Johnsville, Bradley county, Ark.
50  Charles Nevills, L. I., teacher, Jefferson county, Ark.
51  Luella V. Allen, L. I., teacher, Hot Springs, Ark.
52  Joseph Rose, L. I., Fort Smith, Ark.
53  James H. Vickers, L. I., teacher, Dermott, Ark.
54  Robert N. Davis, L. I., minister, Dermott, Ark.

## 1892.

55  Mary F Barnett, L. I., teacher, Warren, Ark.
56  *Julia A. Cook, L. I., teacher, Bonham, Texas.
57  James H. Fort, L. I., teacher, Jefferson Springs, Ark.
58  Frank H. Wright, L. I., teacher, Nashville, Tenn.
59  Perry L. Bailey, L. I., teacher, Desha county, Ark.
60  John H. Harrison, L. I., A. B. Wilmar, Ark.
61  W W Jones, L. I., teacher, Columbia county, Ark.
62  James W Miller, L. I., teacher, Jefferson county, Ark.
63  Allen N Freeman, L. I., teacher, Pine Bluff, Ark.
64  George W Sanders, L. I., Pine Bluff Postoffice, Jefferson county, Ark.

## 1893.

65  Marion F Harris, L. I., teacher, Camden, Ark.
66  Allen W Patterson, L. I., teacher, Stephens, Ark.
67  James C. Young, L. I., teacher, Baxter, Ark.
68  Josie Pierce, L. I., teacher, Dermott, Ark.

159

69   Charles S. Williams, L. I., teacher, Phillips county, Ark.

## 1 8 9 4

70   Edna Brown, L. I., teacher, Jefferson county, Ark.
71   Jeremiah Townsend, L. I., teacher, Kedron, Ark.
72   Silas J. Altheimer, L. I., principal, Dardanelle, Ark.
73   Edward Craigin, L. I., principal, Newport, Ark.
74   Amanda Davis, L. I., missionary, Monrovia, Liberia.
75   John R. Dykes, L. I., teacher, El Dorado, Ark.
76   Thomas J. Robinson, L. I. teacher, Kedron, Ark.

## 1 8 9 5

77   John Berry, L. I., teacher, Linwood, Ark.
78   John W Stuart, L. I., teacher, Stewart's Chapel, Ark.
79   Thomas C. Green, L. I., Washington, D. C.
80   Walker Hill, L. I., teacher, Nashville, Ark.
81   William D. Herron, L. I., teacher, Glenville, Ark.
82   Irene V Coleman, L. I., teacher, Pine Bluff, Ark.
83   David Davis, L. I., Pine Bluff, Ark.
84   James Fox, L. I., teacher, Cotton Plant, Ark.
85   Thomas M. Walton, L. I., teacher, Mineral Springs, Ark.
86   Leland Patillo, L. I., Pine Bluff, Ark.
87   Alonzo Shanks, L. I., Local, Pine Bluff Herald, Pine Bluff, Ark.

## 1 8 9 6

88   Mary E. Moore, L. I., teacher, Pine Bluff, Ark.
89   Andrew H. Hill, L. I., minister, Wilberforce, Ark.
90   Sarah E. Murphy, L. I., teacher, Texarkana, Ark.
91   Ozro I. Moppin, A B., teacher, De Witt, Ark.
92   Ida L. Moon, L. I., Pine Bluff, Ark.
93   Charles S. Duke, L. I., Pension Department, Washington, D. C.

## 1 8 9 7

94   Minnie Holly, L. I., teacher, Fayetteville, Ark.
95   Z. M. Mazique, L. I., teacher, Pastoria, Ark.
96   Agnes Greene, L. I., Pine Bluff, Ark.
97   Elizabeth L. Moore, L. I., Pine Bluff, Ark.
98   Churchill H. Stuart, L. I , Stewart's Chapel, Ark.
99   Mamie M. Scott, L. I., Pine Bluff, Ark.
100  Wilson S. Jones, L. I., principal, Forest City, Ark.

## 1 8 9 8

101  Irving M. Bass, L. I., teacher, Horatio, Ark.
102  Philip H. Bush, L. I., clerk, Pine Bluff, Ark.
103  Sarah A. Haynes, L. I., principal, Fulton, Ark.
104  Chas. S. Oats, L. I., clerk, Pine Bluff, Ark.
105  Leonora Powers, L. I., teacher, Pocahontas, Ark.
106  Brown J Porter, L. I., clerk, Pine Bluff, Ark.
107  Claud H. Thomas, L. I., clerk, Pine Bluff, Ark.
108  Wiley Wilson, L. I., clerk, Pine Bluff, Ark.
109  Joseph A. Winters, L. I., teacher, England, Ark.

## 1 8 9 9 .

110  Addie Diamond, L. I., teacher, Texarkana, Ark.
111  Bertha J. Jefferson, L. I., teacher, Jefferson county, Ark.

112 Edward Greene, L. I., Texarkana, Ark.
113 S. E. Edwards, L. I., Texarkana, Ark.
114 Mattie Harper, L. I., teacher, Grace, Ark.
115 S. S. Greene, L. I., teacher, Wrightsville, Ark.
116 John C. Cook, L. I., teacher, Wrightsville, Ark.
117 Lavinia McKay, L. I., Little Rock, Ark.
118 J E. Ashmore, L. I., teacher Ashvale. Ark.
119 *J W Cothrine, L. I., teacher, Batesville, Ark.
120 Minnie Taylor, L. I., teacher, Pine Bluff, Ark.
121 Hamilton Offord, L. I., teacher, Pine Bluff, Ark.
122 Wm. O. T Watkins, L. I., principal, Batesville, Ark.
123 *Sadie Battle, L. I., teacher, Pine Bluff, Ark.
124 O. Benj. Jefferson, L. I., teacher, Arkansas City, Ark.

*Deceased.

---

# APPOINTMENTS.

The following list shows the names and counties of the appointees in attendance during the school year 1900-1901

ARKANSAS—Jasper Fluker, Peter Flowers, P S. Hill, N Johnson, Addie Diamond, A. J. Ferguson, M. M. Mason, Arris Rutledge, Lucinda Moore, O. I. Moppin, M. Flowers.
BRADLEY—A. Hammond.
CALHOUN—J W McCray, Gus McCray, J. H. Hegler, Samuel Davis.
CLEVELAND—Miles Frazier, Felix Tolefree.
COLUMBIA—John Burton, Wm. Peters, Dover Greene, Robert Hanson, John Johnson, Seeby Bagby.
CHICOT—Malinda Harding, Wm. Triplett, Fannie Jamison, Cynthia Wilson, Nicie Stewart.
CRITTENDEN—R. B. Pearson.
CONWAY—Sidney Hines, Junior Hines.
DESHA—Geo. Baily, DeWitt Bailey, Susan Howard, O. B. Jefferson, Finley Crane.
DREW—Joseph McDaniels, Cora Davis, C. A. Coleman.
DALLAS—R. E. Hughes, John Perry, G. W Smith.
FRANKLIN—Orelius Shepherd, Wm Carter, Dudley Smith, L. F Gardner
FAULKNER—L. Woodard, Carrie Simpson, Choney Thompson.
GARLAND—Carrie McGavock.
GRANT—H. I Mays.
HOT SPRINGS—James Franklin.
HEMPSTEAD—Paul L. Johnson.
HOWARD—M. F. Hicks.
JEFFERSON—W O. T Watkins, J N Cothrine, Agnes Greene, C. H. Walker, S. M. McPherson, Leslie Pierce, H. Ellis, A. A. Shanks, Joseph Daniels, Chas. Epperson, L. Shaw, William Jackson, Samuel Green, Beulah Johnson, W Whiteside, Wm. Moore, Robert Pleasant, Martin Pleasant, Rosa Gordon, C. H. Thomas, Nettie B. Hollis, Mary Johnson, Indiana Harvell, Martha Litzey, Marcus Murchison, Susan Jacko, Maud Thomas, Emma Thompson, Sarah Billingsby, John Freeman, Laura Patterson, Florina Webb, J C. Freeman, W. T. Winston, Felix Coleman, James Williams, L. McKay, Alice Frazier, K. Williams, I. Smith, Frank Bankhead, Willie Thomas, G. B. White, William Wooten, Mattie

Harper, Robert Adams, Mattie Coleman, Hamilton Offord, S. Battle, Bertha Jefferson, B. Williams, Jamie Jones, Bessie Woolfolk, C. C. Shanks, G. Brown, A. Caruthers, Fannie Johnson, Rosa Grundy, Willie Wilson, Sammie Williams, Harry Porter, D. T Ward, William Scott.
LAFAYETTE—Minnie Connor, Abram Murray, Newton Haynes, Rena High, J. H. Germany, A. Harbor, T. W. Givens, Dover Holmes.
LOGAN—John Q. Byrd, Reuben Byrd, Ernest Byrd.
LINCOLN—Mary Hood, James Moore, Mack Scarver
LONOKE—W. L. Taylor, Joseph Mercer.
LEE—Frank Smith, Frank Wright.
MONROE—Minnie Taylor, W. H. VanBuren, L. Jackson, J H. Davis, Isaac Phillips, Isaac Curry.
MILLER—P. H. Bush, C. S. Oats, S. E. Edwards.
MISSISSIPPI—Fannie Head.
NEVADA—Maryland Key.
POPE—T A. Ross.
PHILLIPS—Sidney Thornton, Ladora Russell, T Hutchins, P. Hutchins, Carrie Jones, M. Walker, William Rambo.
PULASKI—Edward Green, Annie London, J E. Ashmore, S. L. Ashmore, G. Ezell, John Cook, Emma Cook, Ella Cook, A. J Taylor, Arthur Hicks, Elizabeth Walters, W. Walters.
ST. FRANCIS—Francis Wamble.
SALINE—Fred T Jones.
UNION J L. Scott, G. L. Scott, A. Hardy, W Howard, A. L. McElroy, S. L. Cook, R. B. Johnson.
VAN BUREN—William Williams.
WOODRUFF—Grant Watson.
WHITE—Robert Nelson, John H. Wright.

---

# CATALOGUE OF STUDENTS,

*For the Year Commencing September 3, 1899, and Ending June 3, 1900.*

## COLLEGIATE DEPARTMENT

### SENIOR.

| | | |
|---|---|---|
| Cook, John | Wrightsville | Pulaski |
| Green, Agnes | Pine Bluff | Jefferson |
| Oats, Charles S. | Texarkana | Miller |

### SOPHOMORE

| | | |
|---|---|---|
| Cartright, Grace | Pine Bluff | Jefferson |
| Ferguson, Arthur J. | Casscae | Arkansas |
| Frazier, Alice | Pine Bluff | Jefferson |
| Flowers, Peter P. | Mt. Adams | Arkansas |
| Head, Fannie | Monroe, La. | |
| Hutchison, Peyton | Locust Bayou | Phillips |
| Hutchison, Thomas | " | " |
| Shanks, Albert | Pine Bluff | Jefferson |
| Smith, Irene | Warren | " |
| Van Buren, W. M. | Clarendon | Monroe |

162

| NAME | POSTOFFICE | COUNTY |
|------|-----------|--------|
| Williams, William | Cleveland | Conway |
| Wilson, Willie | Pine Bluff | Jefferson |
| Woodard, James S. | Conway | Faulkner |
| Wright, John H. | Newport | Jackson |

## FRESHMAN

| | | |
|------|-----------|--------|
| Bagby, Seeby | Magnolia | Columbia |
| Cook, Ella | Wrightsville | Pulaski |
| Cole, Mollie | Hope | Hempstead |
| Craig, Luna | Pine Bluff | Jefferson |
| Dedman, J Oscar | El Dorado | Union |
| Ellis, Henrietta | Pine Bluff | Jefferson |
| Gordon, Rosa | Pastoria | " |
| Harville, Indiana | Pine Bluff | " |
| Hawkins, Collins | Richmond | Little River |
| Hill, P Solomon | Hensley | Jefferson |
| Hegler, John H. | Cotton Belt | Calhoun |
| Litzey, Martha | Pine Bluff | Jefferson |
| Mason, Minnie M | Stuttgart | Arkansas |
| Mosley, Lucy | Newport | Jackson |
| McPherson, M Samuel | Linwood | Jefferson |
| McElvene, Eliza | Hope | Hempstead |
| Simpson, Carrie | Conway | Faulkner |
| Strong, Edward E. | Hope | Hempstead |
| Smith, Frank | Mariana | Lee |
| Taylor William | Stuart Chapel | Jefferson |
| Wamble, Frances | Pine Bluff | |
| Wilson, Cynthia | Lake Village | Chicot |
| White, Grant B. | Pastoria | Jefferson |
| " | | |

## SUB-FRESHMAN

| | | |
|------|-----------|--------|
| Bailey, DeWitt | Arkansas City | Desha |
| Billingsley, Sallie | Corner Stone | Jefferson |
| Byrd, Reuben M. | Paris | Logan |
| Caruthers, Alice | Pine Bluff | Jefferson |
| Coleman, Mattie | " " | " |
| Davis, Cora | Montongo | Drew |
| Elrod, Alene | Scotts | Lonoke |
| Frazier, Miles | Toledo | Cleveland |
| Hammond, Albert | Warren | Bradley |
| Harbor, Allen A. | Walnut Hill | Lafayette |
| Holmes, Dover | Magnolia | Columbia |
| Johnson, Fannie | Pine Bluff | Jefferson |
| Johnson, Mary | Crockett, Texas | |
| Jamison, Hugh | Dermott | Chicot |
| Jones, Fred T | El Dorado | Union |
| Jones, Jassie | Pastoria | Jefferson |
| Johnson, John | Magnolia | Columbia |
| McElroy, Allen | Smackover | Union |
| Moore, Jas. W. | Walnut Lake | Lincoln |
| Offord, Andrew | Pine Bluff | Jefferson |
| Parks, Joshua | Paris | Logan |
| Shaw, Lucy | Pastoria | Jefferson |
| Williams, Blanchard J. | Linwood | " |

163

## PREPARATORY DEPARTMENT.

### A CLASS.

| NAME | POSTOFFICE | COUNTY |
|---|---|---|
| Adams, Robert. | | |
| Bankhead, Frank | Pine Bluff | Jefferson |
| Bryant, Alfred | Mariana | Lee |
| Byrd, John | Paris | Logan |
| Byrd, Ernest. | | |
| Burton, J. E. | Magnolia | Columbia |
| Bolden, David | El Dorado | Union |
| Cook, Edward | " | " |
| Crane, Finley | Red Bluff | Desha |
| Dickerson, David | Texarkana | Miller |
| Epperson, Chas. | Fairfield | Jefferson |
| Flowers, John | Mt. Adams | Arkansas |
| Fluker, Jasper | Arkansas City | Desha |
| Germany, Jas. H. | Cotton Belt | Lafayette |
| Griffin, Hattie | Portland | Ashley |
| Hughes, Robert | | Grant |
| Hayes, Newton | Lewisville | Lafayette |
| Harris, Vienna | Rison | Cleveland |
| Hollis, Nettie B. | Altheimer | Jefferson |
| Harper, Elizabeth | El Dorado | Union |
| Harper, Walter G. | Magnolia | Columbia |
| Hansom, Robert | | " |
| Hicks, Arthur | Ashvale | Pulaski |
| Knight, Matthew | Pine Bluff | Jefferson |
| Kennedy, Jas. A. | Cotton Plant | Woodruff |
| McDaniel, Joseph | Monticello | Drew |
| McDonal, Joseph | Magnolia | Columbia |
| Mays, Henry I. | " | " |
| Mills, Joseph | " | " |
| Moore, William | Linwood | Jefferson |
| Nelson, Robert | Searcy | White |
| Oglesby, Julia | Monticello | Drew |
| Porter, Harry. | Pine Bluff | Jefferson |
| Pleasant, Robert. | Linwood | " |
| Rutledge, Arris. | Ethel | Arkansas |
| Smith, Jno. W. | Moticello. | Drew |
| Stewart, Nicie | Lake Village | Chicot |
| Studymir, Major | Van Buren | Crawford |
| Taylor, Anderson | Ashvale | Pulaski |
| Taylor, Arthur | | Phillips |
| Thompson, Anthony | Magnolia. | Columbia |
| Thompson, Choney L. | Conway | Faulkuer |
| Thompson, Emma | Pine Bluff | Jefferson |
| Thornton, Sidney. | Wrightville | Pulask |
| Triplett, W. M. | Lake Village | Chicot |
| Vance, Levi. | | Phillips |
| Wilson, John B. | Lake Village | Chicot |
| Wilson, Rachel | " | " |
| Winston, Willie | Pine Bluff | Jefferson |
| Williams, James | Linwood | " |
| Williams, Malisie | Pine Bluff | " |

Whiteside, Wilkins ...  Noble......  .....      "
Walker, Charles.

### B CLASS.

Burks, Cora...... .....Pine Bluff ... ...Jefferson
Bowie, Ezekiel..........Helena. .........Phillips
Byrd, John B. .........  Paris ...  .... ..Logan
Brown, Mary  .......Lake Village . ..Chicot
Bolden, Adaline.. ...... El Dorado. .   ...Union
Barnett, Ida .. ...... .. New Edinburgh  Cleveland
Culliver, Vanetta ......Pine Bluff ...  .Jefferson
Curray, Isaac .. ..... . Clarendon ..... Monroe
Cartright, Thomas ..... Pine Bluff .... .Jefferson
Ezell, Tassy  .....  .....Little Rock. ... . Pulaski
Flowers, Mary . .......Mt. Adams .. .. .Arkansas
Frazure, Lydia . ......................Cleveland
Freeman. Jacob.........Altheimer ......Jefferson
Harding, Malinda. ....Lake Village ... Chicot
Hunter, Walter  ......Dermott...... .Chicot
Hurd, Carrie  . ......Hensley ... .. Saline
Hines, Junior .. ...... Conway  ... Faulkner
Horbor, John J .. ......Walnut Hill ..  Lafayette
Johnson, Beulah .... ...Sedalia, Mo.
Johnson, Paul L. ......Magnolia. ... Columbia
Johnson, Maria .. .. .. Lake Village .. Chicot
Jacko, Susie ...  .. ...Pine Bluff  Jefferson
Jackson, Jas. H. .. ...   "  .. ....  "
Jackson, Leetta  .... . Indian Bay  . ..Monroe
Lightfoot, Sarah .... . Lake Village  . .Chicot
Murray, James  . .Corner Stone ..Jefferson
Martin, Ophelia  .... .Pine Bluff  ... .Jefferson
Maxwell, Jackson  . .. Bebee .........White
Murchison, John M. .. Rison ..... ...Cleveland
Mercer, Joseph . .. .Kes . ..... ..Lonoke
McCra, Isom...,...... .. .... ..... ..Calhoun
Morgan, Isaac ...... ..Ladd.. .... '. Lincoln
Oliver, Everett.. ..... .Pine Bluff .. ...Jefferson
Powell, Mary . ......... "  "  ... ... "
Patterson, Monroe................ Chicot
Paschal, Alonza .... ...Marianna ... .. Lee
Penning, Francis .... ..Warren  ... . Bradley
Ryan, Icyphene .. ... Casscas ... .. .Arkansas
Ryan, Thomas . .. ...   "  "  ... .. "
Shumpert, B. Wickliff .Varner . . .....Lincoln
Smith, Frank........ ..Marianna. ......Lee
Thomas, Maud .. .. .Pine Bluff...... Jefferson
Taffe, Stella. .... . . .. .. ...  ...Little River
Williams. Sammie . . .Pine Bluff ... ..Jefferson
Watt, Vina .......... ..Conway .........Faulkner
Woodard, Luther  ..   "  "  .. "
Webb, Florina .........Wabbaseeca .. ...Jefferson

### C CLASS.

Bradford, Ed.
Brown, Whitty ........ .Conway ....... ..Faulkner
Boyce, Susia.... ..... Indian Bay .....Monroe
Camp, Eddie  .........Pine Bluff........Jefferson

| NAME | POSTOFFICE | COUNTY |
|---|---|---|
| Claiborne, Rebecca . | Portland | Ashley |
| Cowser, Robert. | | |
| Dennie, Cora | . Jonesboro . | Craighead |
| Devenport, Isaac. . | ..Portland . . | Ashley |
| Dixon, Joseph .... | Pine Bluff . | Jefferson |
| Evans, Chas. . . | Rison | Cleveland |
| Fluker, Soloman .. .. | Arkansas City | ..Desha |
| Greene, Dozier . . . | Magnolia. . . | ..Columbia |
| Gilmore, Blanche . . | Pine Bluff | .Jefferson |
| Gardner, George .. | ..Horatio | ..Desha |
| Glass, Minnie . | .....Indian Bay | .... Monroe |
| Hockenhull, Malinda | Wabbaseca | .. .Jefferson |
| Hooks, Harvey .. . | Magnolia . | Columbia |
| Holloway, Jennie .. . | ..Cero Gordo | Little River |
| Horbor, Ellis . | ..Walnut Hill | Lafayette |
| Hale, Pauline . . . | Pine Bluff .. | Jefferson |
| Hutchinson, Mattie | Lake Village | Chicot |
| Ishmon, James | | |
| London, Annie | Little Rock | .Pulaski |
| Lightfoot, Peter | Lake Village | ..Chicot |
| Lightfoot, Isiah | " " | " |
| Lightfoot, Alex | " | " |
| Mills, Levi . | .Van Buren | Crawford |
| Miller, London | Newport | Jackson . |
| Moore, . | .Ethel . .. | Arkansas |
| Moore, Beersheba | . " | " |
| Motley, Ella * | .Pointer | .Jefferson |
| O'Neal, Harvey . | .Lake Village . | Chicot |
| Pointer, De Grace | .Pointer . . | Jefferson |
| Patterson, Dorlister . | . Laconia . . | Desha |
| Ramsey, Wm J .. .. | .Horatio . . . | Little River |
| Richmond, Blanche | .Pine Bluff . | Jefferson |
| Rucker, Vassie ... .. | " " | " |
| Royal, Lydia.. .. | ..Lake Village . | Chicot |
| Sturgen, Elisha | .Noble | ...Jefferson |
| Stokes, Mollie | Parkdale | Ashley |
| Smith, Emma | Avenue | Phillips |
| Starks, Mary | Lake Village | Chicot |
| Tyler Courtney | .Indian Bay | .Monroe |
| Tate, Loura . | ..Humphrey | . Jefferson |
| William, Charles | . . . . | Desha |
| Ward, James .. | Pine Bluff | .Jefferson |
| Winters, Ella | . England .. ... | ' |
| Williams, Laura | . . | " |
| Wilkin, John .. | . ..... .. | Chicot |
| William, James | Portland . | Ashley |
| Walker, Mattie | ....Lake Village | Chicot |

## SEWING DEPARTMENT

| | | |
|---|---|---|
| Cartright, Grace | .Pine Bluff . | .Jefferson |
| Frazier, Alice . | " | " |
| Head, Fannie .. . | " | .. . |
| Smith, Irene . .. ... | " | .. |
| Wilson, Willie .. ...... | " | ........ . |
| Craig, Luna............. | " | ....... . |

166

| NAME | POSTOFFICE | COUNTY |
|---|---|---|
| Ellis, Henrietta . | " | " |
| Harvill, Indiana . . | " | " |
| Litzsey, Martha... . | " | " |
| Wamble, Frances . ... | " | " |
| Corruthers, Alice .... . | " | " |
| Coleman, Mattie . . | " | " |
| Johnson, Fannie .. ... | " | " |
| Hollis, Nettie .. . . | " | " |
| Rose, Hettie .. . | " | " |
| Thompson, Emma .... | " | " |
| Williams, Malissa.. . | " | " |
| Greene, Agnes .. . | " | " |
| Gordon, Rosa. . .... | Pastoria. . | " |
| Billingsly, Sallie . .....Cornerstone . . | " |
| Elrod, Allene ..... ...Scotts.... . .... | " |
| Shaw, Lucy ........ ...Pastoria.. .... | " |
| Jones, Jannie . ..... " . ...... . | " |
| Cole, Mollie . ...Hope . ., . | . Hempstead |
| Cook, Ella. . .... Wrightsville | ..Pulaski |
| Mason, Minnie . . . Stuttgart . ; | Arkansas |
| McElvene, Eliza .....Hope ...: | . Hempstead |
| Mosley, Lucy .... . . Newport | .Jackson |
| Simpson, Carrie. . Conway ..:. | Faulkner |
| Wilson, Cynthia . Lake Village | Chicot |
| Davis, Cora . Montongo | Drew |
| Johnson, Mary Crockett, Texas | |
| Griffin, Hattie Parkdale | Ashley |
| Harris, Vienna. . Kedron | Cleveland |
| Harper, Elizabeth. . El Dorado , | Union |
| Oglesby, Julia .Monticello : | Drew |
| Stewart, Nicey .. .Lake Village | ...Chicot |
| Wilson, Rachel ... . " | " |
| Thompson, Choney:. ..Conway | . Faulkner |

## TYPEWRITING DEPARTMENT

| | | |
|---|---|---|
| Cartwright, Grace . Pine Bluff | .Jefferson |
| Craig, Luna. . | " | " |
| Frazier, Alice . | " | " |
| Wilson, Willie .. . | " | " |
| Ellis, Henrietta . | " | " |
| Harvill, Indiana . | " | " |
| Litzsey, Martha . . | " | " |
| Wamble, Frances | " | " |
| Caruthers, Alice | " | " |
| Coleman, Mattie . .. | " | " |
| Johnson, Fannie | " | " |
| Hollis, Nettie | " | " |
| Rose, Hettie . | " | " |
| Williams, Mellissa .. " | " |
| Greene, Agnes .. . | " | " |
| Gordon, Rosa .Pastoria . . | " |
| Billingsley Sallie Cornersones .... . | " |
| Elrod, Alene .. . Scotts .. ..... | " |
| Shaw, Lucy ......Pastoria......... | " |
| Jones, Jannie ....... . " .......... | " |

| NAME | POSTOFFICE | COUNTY |
|---|---|---|
| Head, Fannie | Monroe, La. | |
| Smith, Irene | Warren | Bradley |
| Cole, Mollie | Hope | Hempstead |
| Cook, Ella | Wrightsville | Pulaski |
| Mason, Minnie | Stuttgart | Arkansas |
| McElvene, Eliza | Hope | Hempstead |
| Moseley, Lucy | Newport | Jackson |
| Simpson, Carrie | Conway | Faulkner |
| Wilson, Cynthia | Lake Village | Chicot |
| Davis, Cora | Montongo | Drew |
| Johnson, Mary | Crockett, Texas. | |
| Griffin, Hattie | Portland | Ashley |
| Harris, Vina | Kedron | Cleveland |
| Harper, Elizabeth | El Dorado | Union |
| Oglesby, Julia | Monticello | Drew |
| Stewart, Nicey | Lake Village | Chicot |
| Thompson, Emma | Conway | Faulkner |
| Wilson, Rachel | Lake Village | Chicot |

## LIST OF STUDENTS IN THE SHOPS.

| | | | |
|---|---|---|---|
| Charles Walker, | James Williams, | Jasper Fluker, | Matthew Knight, |
| Jos. McDaniel, | Chas. Oates, | Robt. Nelson, | Alex Sturdemeyer, |
| William Byrd, | John Cook, | Robt. Pleasant, | Frank Bankhead, |
| Andrew Offord, | Sealy Bagby, | Wm. Taylor, | Sidney Thornton, |
| John Moore, | Joshua Parks, | John Byrd, | Albert Hammond, |
| Levi Vance, | Arthur Taylor, | John Flowers, | Robt. Hanson, |
| Robt. Adams, | Harry Porter, | Albert Shanks, | William Winston, |
| J H. Wright, | A. J. Ferguson, | Thos. Hutchins, | Peyton Hutchins, |
| Peter Flowers, | Chas. Epperson. | Wm. Triplett, | Walter Harper, |
| Ernest Byrd, | Arthur Hicks, | Arris Rutledge, | Wilkins Whiteside |
| A. J Taylor, | Edward Cook, | Finley Crane, | J H. Burton, |
| DeWitt Bailey, | Hugh Jamison, | E. E. Strong, | Fred Jones, |
| B. J Williams, | Oscar Dedman, | Joseph Mills, | James Kennedy, |
| Jos. Wilson, | D. B. Bolden, | Alfred Bynant. | |

## RECAPITULATION.

| | Males, | | Females, | | Total, | |
|---|---|---|---|---|---|---|
| Collegiate | 2 | | 1 | | 3 | |
| Normal | 34 | " | 26 | " | 60 | |
| Preparatory | 95 | " | 57 | " | 152 | |
| Sewing Department. | | | 39 | " | 39 | |
| Typewriting | | | 39 | " | 39 | |
| Mechanical | 55 | " | | " | 55 | |
| Total in all Departments | 186 | | 162 | | 348 | |
| Less number counted twice | | | | | 133 | |
| | | | | | 215 | |

## CALENDAR.

Opening .....................................First Monday in September
Examination—First week in September ; Third week in January and May
Closing—..............................................First week in June.
Commencement—............................First Tuesday in June, 8 p. m.
Exhibits—Shops, Needlework, Typewriting and Drawing:
          First Wednesday in June, 10 a. m. to 3 p. m.
Alumni Association—................... First Wednesday in June, 10 a. m.
Reunion—............................... First Thursday in June, 8 p. m.

# COURSE OF STUDY.

## PREPARATORY DEPARTMENT

### FIRST YEAR.

FIRST TERM—Monteith's Comprehensive Geography, Anderson's United States History; Reed and Kellogg's Graded Lessons in English, Robinson's Shorter Course Arithmetic; Penmanship, Spencerian or Eclectic; Drawing, Forbriger; Analysis, Swinton, Vocal Music, Tonic Sol-Fa.

SECOND TERM—Geography, Monteith, Graded Lessons in English, Reed and Kellogg; Arithmetic, Robinson's Shorter Course; Penmanship, Spencerian; Drawing, Forbriger; United States History, Anderson, Analysis, Swinton; Vocal Music.

THIRD TERM—Geography, Monteith, Graded Lessons in English. Reed and Kellogg; Penmanship, Spencerian, Drawing, Forbriger, Arithmetic, Robinson; United States History, Anderson, Analysis, Swinton, Vocal Music.

### SECOND YEAR

FIRST TERM—Geography, Monteith, Arithmetic, Robinson; Penmanship, Spencerian or Eclectic; United States History; Swinton's Analysis, Vocal Music.

SECOND TERM—Geography, Monteith; Graded Lessons in English, Reed and Kellogg, Arithmetic, Robinson; Penmanship, Spencerian or Eclectic, Drawing, Forbriger, Anderson's United States History, Swinton's Analysis, Vocal Music.

THIRD TERM—Monteith's Geography, United States History, Anderson, Graded Lessons in English, Reed and Kellogg, Arithmetic, Robinson, Penmanship, Spencerian or Eclectic, Drawing, Forbriger; Analysis, Swinton.

### THIRD YEAR

FIRST TERM—Analysis, Swinton, Arithmetic, Robinson, Graded Lessons in English, Reed and Kellogg, General History, Anderson, Physical Geography, Houston, Latin, Collier and Daniels, Typewriting.

SECOND TERM—Analysis, Swinton; Higher Lessons in English, Reed and Kellogg, Physiology, Hutchinson, General History, Anderson, Physical Geography, Houston, Typewriting.

THIRD TERM—General History, Anderson, Higher Lessons in English, Reed and Kellogg; Algebra, Wilson; English Composition, Chittenden; Physical Geography, Houston; Typewriting.

## COURSE OF STUDY--Continued.

*1—Normal Course for Licentiate of Instruction.* ( L I.)

| Classes | FIRST TERM | SECOND TERM | THIRD TERM |
|---|---|---|---|
| A Class | English | English | English |
| | Typewriting, Shop Work | Typewriting, Shop Work | Typewriting, Shop Work |
| | Arithmetic | Arithmetic | Arithmetic |
| | Geography | United States History | United States History |
| | Reading and Spelling (optional) | Reading and Spelling (optional) | School Law |
| | Latin | Latin | Latin |
| Sub-Freshman Class | Ed. Chemistry (optional) | Pedagogics | |
| | Typewriting, Shop Work | Typewriting, Shop Work | Typewriting, Shop Work |
| | Pedagogics | Elementary Botany (optional) | Elementary Physiology |
| | Geometry | Algebra | Algebra |
| | Latin or Phys. Geography | Latin or Phys. Geography and Book keeping | Latin or Book-keeping |
| | English | English | Constitution of Arkansas |
| Freshman Class | Algebra | Algebra and Geometry | Geometry |
| | Typewriting, Shop Work | Typewriting, Shop Work | Typewriting, Shop Work |
| | English | English | English or Physics |
| | | History of Education | School Management |
| | Physics | Physics (optional) | Zoology  optional |
| | Latin | Latin | Latin |
| Sophomore Class | Typewriting, Shop Work | Typewriting, Shop Work | Typewriting, Shop Work |
| | General History | General History or Surveying (optional) | General History including Constitution of U. S. |
| | Latin | Latin | Latin |
| | General Chemistry | General Chemistry | Psychology |
| | Astronomy | Astronomy | Astronomy |
| | | Science of Education | Const. and School Law |
| | Geometry | Plane Trigonometry | Ethics  optional |

# COURSE OF STUDY--Concluded.

## 2—Classical Course for Bachelor of Arts. (B. A.)

| Classes | FIRST TERM | SECOND TERM | THIRD TERM |
|---|---|---|---|
| A Class | English | English | English |
| | Arithmetic | Arithmetic | Arithmetic |
| | Geography | United States History | United States History |
| | Reading and Spelling (optional) | Reading and Spelling (optional) | Reading and Spelling (optional) |
| | Latin | Latin | Latin |
| Sub-Freshman Class | Elementary Zoology (optional) | Elementary Botany (optional) | Book-keeping |
| | Latin | Latin | Latin |
| | Geometry | Algebra | Algebra |
| | Physical Geography | Phys. Geography and Book-keeping | Psychology (optional) |
| | English | English | English |
| Freshman Class | Algebra | Algebra and Geometry | Geometry |
| | English (optional) | English | English |
| | *Greek, °French | °Greek, *French | °Greek, °French |
| | *Physics | *Physics | °Physics |
| | Latin | Latin | Latin |
| Sophomore Class | General History (optional) | General History (optional) | General History |
| | Latin | Latin | Latin |
| | °General Chemistry | °General Chemistry | *General Chemistry |
| | *Greek, °French | °Greek, °French | °Greek, *French |
| | Geometry | Plane Trigonometry | Spher. Trigonometry (optional) |
| Junior Class | *Mineralogy | *Geology | Latin |
| | Analytical Geometry | Analytical Geometry Calculus (optional) | *Calculus |
| | English Literature | English Literature | English Literature |
| | °Latin | Latin | Logic |
| | °Greek, *German | *Greek, °German | °Greek, *German |
| Senior Class | Latin | Latin (optional) | Latin |
| | Anglo-Saxon | Anglo-Saxon | English Philology |
| | *Greek, *Astronomy | °Greek | *Greek |
| | *German | *German, °Surveying | *German |
| | Psychology | Psychology and Ethics | Ethics and Political Economy |

°Of the studies thus marked in each term one is required.
NOTE.—For Mechanical Course see under head of Mechanical Department.

# NORMAL DEPARTMENT.

The design of this Department is to train teachers for the common schools of the state.

Applicants must pass a satisfactory examination in the common English branches in order to pass this Department.

In addition to the thorough knowledge of the branches to be taught, the work comprehends:

1. Training in methods of imparting instruction in the branches to be taught.
2. Method of leading pupils to think and investigate for themselves.
3. How to grade and organize the various kinds of schools.
4. Government or discipline of schools.
5. Duties of teachers as governed by School Law.

## CALENDAR.

The terms commence and end as indicated by the following:

CALENDAR FOR THE SCHOLASTIC YEAR 1900-1901

The Autumn Term will commence September 3, and close December 7, 1900.

The Winter Term will commence December 7, 1900, and close March 4, 1901

The Spring Term will commence March 6, 1901, and close June 7, 1901

HOLIDAYS.

The only holidays given are Christmas, New Year and Thanksgiving days.

---

# APPOINTMENT OF BENEFICIARIES.

By the laws of the State, the appointment of students to the Branch College in numbers from each county in the State, is the same as to the parent University at Fayetteville. The power is vested in the County Courts, but any vacancies occurring during the vacations of the court shall be filled by the Judge of the County Court.

All students thus appointed are entitled to four years' free tuition upon the payment of five dollars matriculation fee, in advance, at the time of entering the school.

All beneficiaries and Normal students should be present at the opening of the Autumn Term; and unnecessary delay, either of old students returning or new ones reporting, will lead to the forfeiture of their appointments. The strictest attention to study, and most exact punctuality in attendance on recitations and other duties, are made the conditions of every student's continuance at the institution. Appointments are not transferable.

The pupils who can be admitted to the Branch Normal College free of tuition are apportioned among the several counties of the State, according to their respective populations, by the United States census of 1890, which apportionment is as follows:

### NUMBER OF BENEFICIARIES.

The number of beneficiaries is limited to one thousand, distributed to the counties of the State in proportion to the population of 1890, and in every case in which a county fails to supply its quota of beneficiaries the Governor is authorized to appoint such beneficiaries to the full number authorized by law; PROVIDED, that such appointment may be vacated on application from a county so failing to fill its quota, but may be resupplied from some other county whose quota has not been filled:

| COUNTIES. | Beneficiaries. | COUNTIES. | Beneficiaries. | COUNTIES. | Beneficiaries. |
|---|---|---|---|---|---|
| Arkansas | 10 | Garland | 11 | Newton | 6 |
| Ashley | 13 | Grant | 8 | Ouachita | 15 |
| Baxter | 7 | Greene | 9 | Perry | 6 |
| Benton | 24 | Hempstead | 24 | Phillips | 28 |
| Boone | 15 | Hot Springs | 10 | Pike | 3 |
| Bradley | 8 | Howard | 12 | Poinsett | 7 |
| Calhoun | 7 | Independence | 21 | Polk | 3 |
| Carroll | 16 | Izard | 14 | Pope | 19 |
| Chicot | 16 | Jackson | 15 | Prairie | 10 |
| Clay | 13 | Jefferson | 29 | Pulaski | 45 |
| Clark | 15 | Johnson | 15 | Randolph | 12 |
| Cleburne | 8 | Lafayette | 6 | Saline | 11 |
| Cleveland | 10 | Lawrence | 10 | Scott | 19 |
| Columbia | 19 | Lee | 16 | Searcy | 7 |
| Conway | 16 | Lincoln | 12 | Sebastian | 28 |
| Craighead | 8 | Little River | 6 | Sevier | 8 |
| Crawford | 11 | Logan | 19 | Sharp | 12 |
| Crittenden | 11 | Lonoke | 15 | Stone | 8 |
| Cross | 6 | Madison | 15 | St. Francis | 10 |
| Dallas | 9 | Marion | 10 | Union | 16 |
| Desha | 11 | Miller | 12 | Van Buren | 11 |
| Drew | 15 | Mississippi | 9 | Washington | 30 |
| Faulkner | 17 | Monroe | 12 | White | 21 |
| Franklin | 18 | Montgomery | 7 | Woodruff | 12 |
| Fulton | 8 | Nevada | 17 | Yell | 18 |

There is also one "Honorary Scholarship" to each county, to be elected for superior merit and proficiency, from the public schools of each county according to section 2, of act of July 23, 1868.

Then annexed notice should be forwarded immediately to the principal of Branch Normal College.

No.                                                                      Arkansas }
                                                                            190    }

To the principal of the Branch Normal College of the Arkansas Industrial University:

I hereby notify you that I have this day appointed
of                                             County, as a student in the Branch Normal College of the Arkansas Industrial University at Pine Bluff.

Given under my hand this           day of                  190

                                                                  County Judge

Printed blanks can be obtained by application to the Principal.

Students are specially requested to procure appointments from their County Judges and bring the same with them. This should, on no account, be neglected.

## EXPENSES.

The expenses of a student at the Branch Normal College need not exceed the amount herein stated.

Board in private families, including, fuel, light and washing, can be had from eight to ten dollars per month. An appointed student pays five dollars entrance fee, which entitles him to free tuition for four years.

Books may be purchased at Pine Bluff at the purchaser's usual retail price.

Quite a number of students have paid a part of their board by labor in private families.

Non-beneficiary students will be charged the sum of one dollar per month for tuition, payable in advance,

The entrance fee must in all cases be paid in advance, and by all students.

## GENERAL STATEMENT.

The Branch Normal College is a department of the Arkansas Industrial University, established pursuant to an act of the General Assembly of the State of Arkansas, approved April 23, 1873, and has been in operation since April 27, 1875. Its primary object is the training of teachers for efficient service in the colored public schools of the State—the law referred to having been enacted with special reference to the "convenience of the poorer classes." For the purpose of carrying out the intent of the law, by enabling those who wish to avail themselves of its advantages, there is no charge for tuition for appointees; the only requirements for admission being suitable age and qualification, appointment from one of the County Judges, and the payment of the entrance fee of five dollars.

### LOCATION, ETC.

The school property consists of a beautiful tract of twenty acres of ground, in the suburbs of Pine Bluff, Jefferson County, Arkansas, and a few rods from the junction of the Missouri Pacific and St. Louis Southwestern Railroads. The school building, completed in 1881, and occupied January 30, 1882, is one of the handsomest edifices in the State, as well as one of the best, being warm and comfortable, well lighted and ventilated. It contains one large assembly room, four recitation rooms, and cloak rooms for males and females. The building is of brick, with slate roof, and trimmings of Alabama granite, and cost, with improvements and furniture, $12,000. The furniture and other equipments are of the best modern styles. The dormitory for females and mechanical buildings are described below.

The Normal Course of study, as will be seen by reference to page 16, is not what goes by that name in many institutions—that is, a mere preparation for teaching the common school branches, but differs from the usual college curriculum merely in the ommission of one or two branches of higher mathematics, and having less in Greek.

The institution is strictly confined, as will be seen from its curriculum, to the higher branches, and children who are not somewhat advanced in the common school branches, are never admitted.

The first two years of the course are intended to rank as the Freshmen and Sophomore years of the usual college curriculum, and the last two years as the equivalent of the Junior and Senior years.

Sixteen classes have graduated in the institution, as will be seen in the list of the Alumni, and are now occupying prominent positions in life.

Recently the entire building has been whitened, painted and repaired, new furniture and an excellent supply of new apparatus purchased.

The reading room has been fitted up in elegant style, and an excellent beginning made toward securing a good library by the collection of about four thousand volumes. It has been supplied with quite a number of valuable newspapers and periodicals, many of which were furnished by their publishers. Among those on file were the Freeman, Indianapolis; Appeal, Minneapolis; Gazette, Huntsville; The Gazette and the Commonwealth, Little Rock; Globe-Democrat and Republic, St. Louis, the Tyler, Detroit, Mich.; Popular Educator, Boston; Lippincott's Educational Quarterly; American Student, New York; Weekly Echo, Pine Bluff; National Baptist, Philadelphia; Southern Review, Helena, Southern School Journal, American Machinist, Scientific American; Nation, Popular Educator, etc.

## THE LIBRARY.

The Library consists of over three thousand five hundred volumes, embracing many valuable reference books, such as Appleton's Cyclopedia, Alden's Cyclopedia, Century Dictionary, Lippincott's Gazeteer, etc. It also has acquired by purchase, during the last years, a fine collection of the works of standard authors—Shakespeare, Milton, Irving, Cooper, Dickens, Longfellow, Carlyle, Tennyson. The library of the Principal, embracing many valuable text and reference books, including the Encyclopædia Brittanica, is also accessible to students. A small collection of minerals, each of which is a typical specimen, and none of which are duplicates, has been procured. A valuable supply of apparatus has been added to the resources of the institution, including an air-pump, electrical machines, barometers, thermometers, induction coils, Geissler's tubes, reagents, etc., also a fine x-ray apparatus.

The Library has also a supply of some of the text-books, which are loaned to the students on deposit of a small fee as security for their return and good usage. The institution gained an award (No. 13,331) from the Chicago Exposition for literary work.

## THE DORMITORY.

The Dormitory for female students is under the supervision of the Principal and his wife. It is a handsome brick structure, sufficient for the accommodation of thirty or forty students. Board bills are payable monthly, in advance, and no deduction is made for loss of time less than one week. Girls staying in the Dormitory are required to keep their own rooms and the halls clean, and to assist, in turn, in the dining-room and kitchen. They are expected to furnish their own bed linen, and are held responsible for all damage to furniture in their rooms. They are not to visit each other's rooms, except by invitation of the occupant, and two are expected to occupy one room. They are not allowed to change rooms, except by permission, nor to visit in town otherwise. The charge for board, fuel and light thus far has been eight dollars per month, in advance, and, if possible, that price will be continued. Students boarding elsewhere are under the supervision of the Principal of the College, and are allowed to board only at places approved by him. The classes in Art, Needlework recite in the Dormitory. Twenty-eight days constitute a month,

Students who cannot comply with the above rules are not desired. This applies especially to advance payment of board.

Parents should send the money for paying board direct to the Principal, and not to the girls; as the latter sometimes use it for other purposes. Parents should require a receipt for board money to be returned at once to them.

Students will not be allowed to remove their property from the Dormitory until their bills are settled in full.

## GENERAL EXERCISES.

In addition to the regular class exercises laid down in the curriculum of study, there are regular lessons in vocal music, which are open to all the students. The general exercises also include a review of the Sabbath school lesson, review of the events of the week, Calisthentics, Music and Drawing. Music upon instruments—the Organ, Piano, Flute, Guitar, etc.—is extra, but very reasonable in price. There are two Literary Societies, the Junior and Senior, which hold weekly meetings and afford excellent opportunities for practice in oratory, debate and composition. It is required that every student shall become a member and attend the meetings of one of the societies, and the failure to perform a duty in the Society subjects the student to the same demerits as in other cases.

The length of the vacation allows the advanced students an opportunity to engage in teaching, and a large proportion of their number have done so during the last five years. In nearly all cases they have given good satisfaction, and conducted their schools with a fair degree of success. The Normal students have also assisted in the work of the institution itself as a part of their training.

As a part of their training, the advanced students of the institution assist in the work of teaching.

It will be a great advantage to the institution if the various County Judges will take a special interest in seeing that their counties are represented. The proper blanks for making appointments will be furnished, together with all necessary information, on application to the Principal, J C. CORBIN, A. M., Pine Bluff, Ark.

## DEPARTMENT OF PLAIN SEWING.

### ART NEEDLEWORK, ETC.

In this Department, the females are trained in Domestic Economy, Plain Sewing, Crocheting, Art Needlework and other pursuits specially suited to their natures; a portion of each day being devoted to these branches and the regular lessons are at the same time attended to. The Department, though only a few years old, has exhibited some fine specimens of work at the State Fair, and received suitable awards for so doing. It has a fine outfit of Singer, Wheeler & Wilson and other sewing machines, besides all other requisites for Embroidery, Drawn Work, Crocheting, etc. Girls employed in this Department soon learn to make their own clothing with taste and economy. Female students have also a thorough training in Type Writing and many of them are quite proficient in the use of the machines.

## DEPARTMENT OF TYPEWRITING,

### SHORTHAND, ETC.

Classes in these branches have one hour's daily practice. Shorthand classes will be formed whenever a sufficient number of students desire to pursue the study. The institution uses the following machines, Smith Premier, Remington and New Century Caligraph.

## NOTICE.

At the close of every term, students who have pursued the studies of the term are entitled to and may receive a printed certificate showing that they have done so, and have passed examination on the same.

Any student claiming to be from the Branch Normal College should be able to show one or more of these certificates, and a failure to do so is almost conclusive evidence that said student has failed in the requisite performance of duty.

The Branch Normal College does not recommend as a teacher any one who does not possess such a printed certificate, signed by the corps of instructors. It is important to notice that these certificates are never issued with any erasures; therefore, if there are any such, they are not the work of the Faculty.

The students mentioned in the foregoing lists are all of advanced grade, and those in the primary department are not received.

Any student faithfully pursuing and completing the Normal Course shall be able to stand the examination for State license to teach.

Section 6166 of the Revised Statutes of the State is as follows: "The State Superintendent of Public Instruction shall have power to grant State certificates, which shall be valid for life, unless revoked, to any person in the State, who shall pass a thorough examination in all those branches required for granting county certificates; and, also, in Algebra and Geometry, Physics, Rhetoric, Mental Philosophy, History, Latin, the Constitution of the United States and of the State of Arkansas, Natural History, and the Theory and Art of Teaching."

It will be observed that the course includes all the branches required for a State certificate in accordance with the law, and in addition, some other subjects with which a teacher should be familiar.

The Branch Normal College has no connection whatever with anything not specified in this catalogue, and any representation to the contrary is false and fraudulent. No student can pass through its curriculum and attain its honors, otherwise than by regular attendance in its classes. It has no connection with any "correspondence" enterprise. It is necessary to make this public statement, as trouble has arisen from persons being under a wrong impression in reference to this matter.

INSTRUCTIONS TO THOSE PREPARING TO BECOME STUDENTS.

The following instructions, if observed, will be of great advantage to any one proposing to become students:

I. Secure an appointment before leaving home, from the County Judge. Failure to do so causes both trouble and expense.

II. Students can enter at any time.

III Do not purchase any new books, but bring along such text-books as you have.

IV The Dormitory for females is distant but a few yards from the junction of the Valley and the Cotton Belt routes, and female students can get off there and afterwards send to the depot for their baggage.

V No student should come to the institution destitute of funds expecting to find employment at once. Many male students work for board, but sometimes it is several weeks before a place can be found. Students need at least enough for entrance fee ($5.00), books and two or three weeks board.

---

## DEPARTMENT OF MECHANIC ARTS.

### FACULTY.

C. E. HOUGHTON,
Superintendent of Mechanic Arts.

W S. HARRIS,
Superintendent and Instructor in Wood Shops.

E. K. BRALEY,
Instructor in Blacksmith and Machine Shops.

LORENZO ELLIS,
Foreman and Engineer.

### EQUIPMENT

BUILDINGS—The shop building was completed in February, 1892. It is of brick, and covers a plot of ground 70x70, comprising a wood shop 70x25, a blacksmith shop 25x25, and a machine shop 35x25. A boiler room 20x25 and a court 35x20 occupy the remaining space.

WOOD SHOP EQUIPMENT—Twelve benches with complete set of carpenter's tools, a double circular-sawing machine, a scroll saw, a buzz planer, a 20" surface-planing machine, a tenoning machine, a mortising and boring machine, six wood-turning lathes, pattern lathe, band-sawing machine, shaper and a hand carving machine.

FORGE SHOP—Twelve Buffalo forges, the blast being supplied by a blower, and the smoke drawn off by a large exhaust fan. Besides the usual outfit of anvils, hammers, tongs, etc., there is a Buffalo punch shear and bar cutter, capable of cutting off 1 inch bar iron, ½x3 inch strap iron, or of punching a hole in ¾ inch iron.

MACHINE SHOP—A 15-inch crank shaper, 24x24x6 feet planer, 20-inch drill press, 15-inch x 2 feet turret lathe, 18 inch x 6 feet engine lathe, 15 inch x by 6 feet engine lathe, Universal milling machine, cutter and reamer grinder, twist mill grinder, power grindstone, and a 70-light dynamo.

HEATING AND POWER PLANT—Power is furnished by two vertical engines, 12-horse power each, steam supplied from two 30-horse power tubular boilers. The piping from feed water is so arranged that the water passes from either pump or injector through a feed water heater to the boilers; and the exhaust piping is so arranged that the exhaust steam from the engines can be used either to heat the feed water or the shops.

WATER SUPPLY—In the court of the shop building is a 4-inch Cook tubular well which will furnish 1,500 gallons of water per hour A Cook pump delivers the water to a tank 40 feet above the ground, holding 10,000 gallons.

SANITARY PROVISIONS—The shops are thoroughly well lighted, ventilated, heated and drained. Sewer connection is made to all buildings, and the abundant water supply is used to insure cleanliness in wash room and water closets.

## GENERAL STATEMENT.

The shops of the Branch Normal College are built and equipped for the purpose of giving the colored boys of our State a chance to make blacksmiths, machinists, and engineers or firemen. The shops will accommodate sixty students at one time, as follows:

| | |
|---|---|
| Wood Shop.......................... .. | 24 |
| Forge Shop.. .......... .. ... ... | 13 |
| Machine Shop...... ..... . ... .. | 16 |
| Tool Rooms..... . ... . . . . | 3 |
| Boiler Room.. .,.. ..... . . . . | 4 |
| | 66 |

While learning the basis of his trade, the student acquires a good knowledge of Language, History, Mathematics and Drawing. Throughout the course of four years in the shops, the student spends an average of ten hours a week in actual labor; and, while the amount of time spent in the shops seems small, experience has shown that students under constant instruction from one exercise to another as soon as the work is well done, makes very rapid progress.

We are therefore prepared to offer·

(a) A course in general shop work extending over three years, followed by a fourth year's work in one of the shops selected by the student. The design is to enable the young man to choose his trade intelligently and to acquire a sound basis for it.

(b) A three years' course in general shop work, followed by a fourth year's work in the management of boilers, engines and heating systems. This course is intended to train young men for practical work of firemen and engineers.

(c) A course in general shop work extending over three years, together with a class-room work in the theory and practice of teaching, followed by a fourth year's work in handling classes in the shops and in laying out series of practical exercise. There are industrial schools for colored boys springing up all over the South, and we hope by this course to help supply the demand for trained shop teachers.

### I. MECHANIC ARTS COURSE.

SECOND TERM—English, 4. Arithmetic, 4. U. S. History, 4. Shop work, wood-turning, cabinet-making, ten hours per week.

THIRD TERM—English, 4. Arithmetic, 4. U. S. History, 4. Shop work, general wood work, ten hours per week.

### SUB-FRESHMAN CLASS.

FIRST TERM—English, 4. Geometry, 4. Physical Geometry, 4. Shop work, setting up machines and saw-fileing, ten hours per week.

SECOND TERM—English, 4. Algebra, 4. Physical Geography and Book keeping, 4. Shop work, management of boilers, forging, ten hours per week.

THIRD TERM—English, 4. Algebra, 4. Book keeping, 4. El. Physiology, 4. Shop work, drawing, welding, tempering, ten hours.

### FRESHMAN CLASS.

FIRST TERM—Algebra, 4. English, 4. Physics, 4. Shop work, chipping and fileing.

SECOND TERM—Algebra and Geometry, 4. English, 4. Physics, 4. Shop work, drilling, turning, ten hours.

THIRD TERM—Geometry, 4. English, 4. Physics, 4. Shop work, planing, ten hours.

### SOPHOMORE CLASS.

FIRST TERM—Geometry, 4. Chemistry, 4. General History, 4. Shop work, ten hours; or care of engines and boilers, ten hours.

SECOND TERM—Plane Trigonometry, 4. Chemistry, 4. General History, 4. Shop work, ten hours; or care of engines and boilers, ten hours.

THIRD TERM—General History, 4. Physcology, 4. Civil Government, 4. Shop work, ten hours; or care of engines and boilers, ten hours.

## II. MANUAL TRAINING, NORMAL COURSE.

### A CLASS.

FIRST TERM—English, 4. Arithmetic, 4. Geography, 4. Shop work, principles of carpentry and joinery, ten hours.

SECOND TERM—English, 4. Arithmetic, 4. U. S. History, 4. Shop work, turning, cabinet making, ten hours.

THIRD TERM—English, 4. Arithmetic, 4. U. S. History, 4. Shop work, pattern-making, ten hours.

### SUB-FRESHMAN CLASS.

FIRST TERM—English, 4. Geometry, 4. Physical Geography, 4. Pedgogics, 4. Shop work, ten hours.

SECOND TERM—English, 4. Algebra, 4. Physical Geography and Book keeping, 4. Pedagogics, 4. Shop work, forging, ten hours.

THIRD TERM—English, 4, Algebra, 4; Book keeping, 4. El. Physiology, 4. Shop work, welding, riveting, tempering, ten hours.

### FRESHMAN CLASS.

FIRST TERM—English, 4. Algebra, 4. Physics, 4. Shop work, clipping and fileing, ten hours.

SECOND TERM—English, 4. Algebra and Geometry, 4. Physics, 4. Hist. Ed., 4. Shop work, drilling, turning, ten hours.

THIRD TERM—English, 4. Physics, 4. School Management, 4. Shop work, planing, milling, ten hours.

SOPHOMORE CLASS.

FIRST TERM—Geometry, 4. General History, 4. Chemistry, 4. Shop teaching, ten hours.

SECOND TERM—Plane Trigonometry, 4. General History, 4. Chemistry, 4. Science of Education, 4. Shop teaching, ten hours.

THIRD TERM—History, 4. Civil Government, 4. School Law, 4. Psychology, 4. Shop teaching, ten hours.

## REMARKS.

Materials and tools will be furnished to students taking shop work. When necessary, however, each student will be expected to provide himself with a blouse and overalls to work in.

In the case of students who are not able to take a regular four years' course, or who have a decided and intelligent preference for a certain kind of shop work, they will be allowed to work in the shop preferred on the following conditions;

1 That, if the student prefers carpentry or blacksmithing, he will be allowed to begin at once. 2. That if he prefers foundry work, he must take bench work, wood-turning, pattern-making, leading up to it. 3. That if he prefers machinist work, he must first learn to forge, weld and temper, in order to make his own tools for the lathe, planer and shaper, and for chipping.

It is urged, however: 1. That students try earnestly to complete the regular course and secure thereby a better education. 2. That the choice of work be made carefully, and those students who have not a decided preference are advised to pursue the regular order of work for the first three years, after which a choice can be made intelligently.

# INSTRUCTORS.

---

J. C. CORBIN, A. M., Ph. D.,
PRINCIPAL.

JAMES C SMITH, A. B,
FIRST ASSISTANT.

THOS G CHILDRESS, A. B,
SECOND ASSISTANT

MRS. ANNA C. FREEMAN, L. I.,
THIRD ASSISTANT.

MISS LOUISA M. CORBIN,
FOURTH ASSISTANT

# Notes

## Chapter 1

1. Ross County (Ohio) Clerk of Court Records, *Black and Mulatto Registration*.

2. J. B. D. DeBow, *Statistical View of the United States Compendium of the Seventh Census* (Washington DC, 1854), 63.

3. Minute Book, First Baptist Church of Chillicothe, David Nickens Heritage Center, Chillicothe, Ohio. Abstracted by Beverly J. Gray. History of First Baptist Church of Chillicothe, Ohio.

4. Ross County, Ohio, *Black and Mulatto Registration*. History of Henrico County, Virginia.

5. Minute Book, First Baptist Church of Chillicothe. Blanche Sydnor White, *First Baptist Church Richmond (Virginia) 1780–1955* (Richmond, VA: Whittet and Shepperson, 1955).

6. Ibid., 38.

7. Ibid., 14.

8. Jeffrey G. Herbert Restored Hamilton County, Ohio Marriages 1860-1869, 51. Federal Population Census, Ohio, 1840, 1850, 1860, 1870.

9. W. P. Dabney, *Cincinnati's Colored Citizens: Historical, Sociological and Biographical* (Cincinnati, OH: Dabney Publishing Co., 1926), 106.

## Chapter 2

1. James J. Burns, *Educational History of Ohio* (Columbus, OH: Historical Publishing Co., 1995), 25.

2. "History of Ohio University," Ohio History Central, http://www.ohiohistorycentral.org/w/Ohio_University?rec=786 (accessed January 12, 2017).

3. Betty Hollow, *Ohio University: The Spirit of a Singular Place 1804-2004* (Athens, OH: University Press, 2004), 15.

4. Ibid., 31.

5. Ibid., 33.

6. "Joseph Carter Corbin, '53," Ohio University Alumni Bulletin, April 1909, 26. Ohio University Catalogue, June 1889.

## Chapter 3

1. W. P. Dabney, *Cincinnati's Colored Citizens: Historical, Sociological and Biographical* (Cincinnati, OH: Dabney Publishing Co., 1926), 21.

2. *African-American Experience in Ohio, 1850-1920.* The Ohio Historical Society, MSS 21713.

3. *The Colored Citizen* (Cincinnati), May 10, 1866.

4. United States Pension Records, Civil War. Roster of Wisconsin Volunteers, War of the Rebellion, 1861–1865, Volume 2, Wisconsin Adjutant General's Office, 772.

## Chapter 4

1. United States Federal Census, 1860.

2. Jeffrey G. Herbert, Restored Hamilton County Ohio Marriages 1860–1869.

3. United States Federal Census, 1880; Oberlin College Preparatory Department Records; Branch Normal College Annual Catalogue, 1900–1901; Waldheim (Forest Home) Cemetery Records.

4. United States Federal Census, 1880, 1900, 1910; *Pine Bluff Daily Graphic*, October 8, 1929; Waldheim (Forest Home) Cemetery Records.

5. United States Federal Census, 1880; Hamilton County, Ohio Burial Records, Volume 9; Union Baptist African American Cemetery, Part 2.

6. United States Census, 1880.

7. United States Federal Census, 1900, 1910; Branch Normal College Catalogue Annual Report 1900–1901.

## Chapter 5

1. Arkansas Free Colored Population, 1860 Bureau of the Census, 15, 507.

2. David Calkins, "Black Education and the 19th Century: An Institutional Analysis of Cincinnati Colored Schools," *Cincinnati Historical Society Bulletin* 33 (Fall 1971): 165.

3. June 23, 1870, *Cincinnati Enquirer*.

4. Mae Najiyyah Duncan, *A Survey of Cincinnati's Black Press & its Editors, 1844–2010* (Xlibris, 2011), 13.

5. Russell E. Bearden, "Pine Bluff (Jefferson County)," Encyclopedia of Arkansas History & Culture, http://www.encyclopediaofarkansas.net/encyclopedia/entry-detail.aspx?entryID=908 (accessed January 2, 2017).

## Chapter 6

1. Thomas Rothrock, "Joseph Carter Corbin and Negro Education in the University of Arkansas," *Arkansas Historical Quarterly* 30 (Winter 1971): 279.

2. Thomas S. Staples, *Reconstruction in Arkansas, 1862–1874* (Gloucester, MA: Peter Smith, 1964), 321.

3. University of Arkansas Board of Trustees Minutes, Branch Normal College Records (MC1921) Box 1, File 3. Special Collections, University of Arkansas Libraries, Fayetteville.

4. Act of Arkansas Number XCVII, 1873, 231–232.

5. Ibid., 233.

6. William J. Simmons, *Men of Mark: Eminent, Progressive and Rising* (Cleveland, OH: Geo M. Rewell & Co., 1887/New York: Arno Press, 1968), 6.

7. Robert A. Leflar, *The First 100 Years: Centennial History of the University of Arkansas* (Fayetteville: University of Arkansas Foundation, Inc., 1972), 274.

8. Rothrock, "Joseph Carter Corbin and Negro Education," 285.

9. *Pine Bluff Republican*, September 2, 1875.

10. Rothrock, "Joseph Carter Corbin and Negro Education," 300.

11. Ibid., 286–287.

12. Corbin's 1876–77 Annual Report, Branch Normal Records (MC-1921), Box 1, File 4. Special Collections, University of Arkansas Libraries, Fayetteville.

13. Ibid.

14. University of Arkansas Trustees Minutes, Box 1, File 3.

15. Rothrock, "Joseph Carter Corbin and Negro Education," 289.

16. C. Fred Williams, "Frustration Amidst Hope: The Land Grant Mission of Arkansas AM&N College, 1873–1972," *Agricultural History* 65, no. 2 (1991): 165.

17. Corbin's Narrative Report to the Board of Trustees for May, 1893, Branch Normal Records, (MC-1921), Box 1, File 4, Special Collections, University of Arkansas Libraries, Fayetteville.

18. Frederick Chambers, "Historical Study of Arkansas Agricultural, Mechanical, and Normal College, 1873–1943," unpublished Ed.D. dissertation, Ball State University, 1970, 107–109.

19. John William Graves, "Negro Disfranchisement in Arkansas," *Arkansas Historical Quarterly* 24 (Summer 1967): 199.

20. Robert A. Leflar, *The First 100 Years*, 273–274.

21. Morrill Land-Grant College Act.

22. Williams, "Frustration Amidst Hope," 115.

23. Izola Preston and Marian Morgan, "Joseph Carter Corbin and the Normal School Movement." *Washington County Historical Society Flashback* 42 (February 1992): 27.

24. Branch Normal College Annual Catalogue 1917-1918.

25. Biographical facts on John Gray Lucas taken from John William Graves, *Town and Country, Race Relations in an Urban-Rural Context, Arkansas, 1865-1905* (Fayetteville: University of Arkansas Press, 1990), 124–125, 150, 157–160, 162, 198.

26. Corbin's Narrative Report to the Board of Trustees for May, 1893, Branch Normal College Records, (MC-1921), Box 1, File 4, Special Collections, University of Arkansas Libraries, Fayetteville.

27. Ibid.

## Chapter 7

1. Corbin's Narrative Report to the Board of Trustees for May, 1893, Branch Normal College Records, (MC-1921), Box 1, File 4, Special Collections, University of Arkansas Libraries, Fayetteville.

2. Ibid.

3. Ibid.

4. John Hugh Reynolds and David Yancey Thomas, *History of the University of Arkansas* (Fayetteville: University of Arkansas Press, 1910), 302.

5. Frederick Chambers, "Historical Study of Arkansas Agricultural, Mechanical, and Normal College, 1873–1943," unpublished Ed.D. dissertation, Ball State University, 1970, 107–109.

## Chapter 8

1. *Pine Bluff Graphic*, January 10, 1911, 8.

2. John W. Cromwell, *The Negro in American History* (Washington DC: The American Negro Academy, 1914), 209.

3. Booker T. Washington, *Up from Slavery: An Autobiography* (Garden City, NY: Doubleday & Company, Inc., 1901), 127.

4. Ibid., 141, 151.

5. Branch Normal College Catalogue and Circular, 1900–1901, 16.


## Chapter 9

1. Thomas Rothrock, "Joseph Carter Corbin and Negro Education in the University of Arkansas," *Arkansas Historical Quarterly* 30 (Winter 1971): 310.

2. Ibid., 311.

3. Ibid.

4. Ibid., 308.


## Chapter 10

1. James P. Brawley, *Two Centuries of Methodist Concern, Bondage, Freedom and Education of Black People* (New York: Vantage Press, 1974), 528.

2. Robert A. Leflar, *The First 100 Years: Centennial History of the University of Arkansas* (Fayetteville: University of Arkansas Foundation, Inc., 1972).

3. Ibid., 310–311.

4. William J. Simmons, *Men of Mark: Eminent, Progressive and Rising* (Cleveland, OH: Geo M. Rewell & Co., 1887/New York: Arno Press, 1968), 832.

5. Ibid.

6. E. M. Woods, "Rev. Joseph A. Booker," *Blue Book of Little Rock and Argenta* (Little Rock, AR: Central Printing Co., 1907), 25–26.

7. Thomas Rothrock, "Joseph Carter Corbin and Negro Education in the University of Arkansas," *Arkansas Historical Quarterly* 30 (Winter 1971): 305.

8. Corbin's Narrative Report to the Board of Trustees for May 1893. Branch Normal College Records (MC-1921), Box 1, File 4, 12-13. Special Collections, University of Arkansas Libraries, Fayetteville.

9. Corbin's Narrative Report to the Board of Trustees, 1893, Branch Normal College Records (MC 1921), Box 1, File 4, 6-7, Special Collections, University of Arkansas Libraries, Fayetteville.

10. Corbin's Narrative Report to the Board of Trustees for May 1893: 2, 5, 6, 9.

11. Denise Malan, "Arkansas Teachers Association (ATA)," Encyclopedia of Arkansas History & Culture, http://www.encyclopediaofarkansas.net/encyclopedia/entry-detail.aspx?entryID=2168 (accessed January 12, 2017).

12. Tribute R. C. Childress (January/February 1992): 3, 30, 31.

13. "Who's Who in Arkansas Freemasonry," PHA; "Masonry in Black Arkansas: History of Prince Hall Masons," Black Footprints Around Arkansas.

14. Freedman's Bank Records, Little Rock, Record #993, April 2, 1873.

15. "History Lovers Take Walk Through History," *Pine Bluff Commercial*, September 7, 2013.

16. "Joseph Carter Corbin," *Who Was Who in America, 1961–1968*, vol. IV (Chicago: A. N. Marquis & Company), 386.

17. *The African-American National Biography*. The dedication mentioned would have been the second Dedication of Union Baptist Church; Union Baptist Church Minutes, 1864–1866, John Parker Research Library, Underground Railroad Freedom Center, Cincinnati; Union Baptist Church Record Book, August 15, 1857–1866.

18. Union Baptist Cemetery (Cincinnati, Ohio).

19. Simmons, *Men of Mark*, 831.

20. National Negro Business League, 78.

21. *Pine Bluff Weekly Graphic*, June 25, 1887.

# Chapter 11

1. William B. Gatewood, *Aristocrats of Color: The Black Elite 1880–1920* (Bloomington: Indiana University Press, 1990), 1, 7, 71.

2. Ibid., 179.

3. Rev. William J. Simmons, *Men of Mark: Eminent, Progressive and Rising* (Cleveland, OH: Geo M. Rewell & Co., 1887/New York: Arno Press, 1968), 44; James W. Leslie, "Ferd Havis: Jefferson County's Black Republican Leader," *Jefferson County Historical Quarterly* 8, no. 1 (1979).

4. William J. Simmons, *Men of Mark: Eminent, Progressive and Rising* (Cleveland, OH: Geo M. Rewell & Co., 1887/New York: Arno Press, 1968), 278–280.

5. Izola Preston and Marian Morgan, "Joseph Carter Corbin and the Normal School Movement," *Washington County Historical Society Flashback* 42 (February 1992):22.

# Chapter 12

1. Isaac Fisher Letter to Mr. B. T. Washington, October 10, 1901.

2. *Our Review Newspaper* 7, no. 5, Little Rock and Pine Bluff, Arkansas (May 1915).

# Chapter 13

1. *Pine Bluff Commercial*, January 12, 1911.

2. "Generations," Holderness Family Genealogy.

3. *The Western Appeal*, January 14, 1911.

4. Ibid.

5. J. C. Corbin Will, Jefferson County Probate Court.

6. "Forest Park and German Waldheim Cemeteries." Historical Society of Oak Park & River Forest, http://www.oprfhistory.org/explore_local_history/foresthome/default.aspx (accessed January 6, 2017).

7. Ursula Bielski and Matt Hucke, *Chicago Graveyards* (Chicago: Lake Claremont Press, 1999), 80, 114.

8. Jefferson County Probate Records for J. C. Corbin, Term 1912, 1913.

9. Ibid.

10. Ibid.

## Chapter 15

1. University of Arkansas Board of Trustees Minutes, Branch Normal College Records, (MC-1921), Box 1, File 3. Special Collections, University of Arkansas Libraries, Fayetteville, 5.

2. Ibid.

3. Corbin's "Narrative Report, 1881-82," Branch Normal College Records (MC-1921), Box 1, File 4. Special Collections, University of Arkansas Libraries, Fayetteville, 1.

4. Ibid.

5. Ibid.; University of Arkansas Board of Trustees Minutes, 6, 7.

6. Ibid., 8.

7. Ibid., 9.

8. Ibid.

9. Thomas Rothrock, "Joseph Carter Corbin and Negro Education in the University of Arkansas," *Arkansas Historical Quarterly* 30 (Winter 1971): 296.

10. University of Arkansas Board of Trustees Minutes, 11.

11. Ibid.

12. Ibid., 12.

13. Ibid.

14. Senate Journal of the State of Arkansas, Twenty-Ninth Session, January 9, 1893. "Report of Committee Visit to the Branch Normal School," 455–456, 458.

15. Ibid.; University of Arkansas Board of Trustees Minutes, 14.

16. Ibid.

17. Ibid.

18. Ibid., 15.

19. Ibid.

20. Ibid., 16.

21. Ibid.

22. Ibid.

23. Ibid.

24. Ibid., 17.

25. Ibid.

26. Ibid.

27. Ibid., 19.

28. Ibid., 18.

## Author's Notes

1. W. E. B. Du Bois, *Black Reconstruction in America* (New York: Athenaeum Press, 1969).

2. John William Graves, *Town and Country: Race Relations and Urban Development in Arkansas, 1865-1905* (Fayetteville: University of Arkansas Press, 1978), 28–29.

# Bibliography

## Manuscript Collections

Black and Mulatto Registration, Clerk of Court, Ross County, Ohio. Branch Normal College Records, Special Collections, University Libraries, University of Arkansas, Fayetteville.

Minutes of the University of Arkansas Board of Trustees, Special Collections, University Libraries, University of Arkansas, Fayetteville.

Minute Book, First Baptist Church, Nickens Heritage Center, Chillicothe, Ohio.

Preparatory Department Records, Oberlin College Library Special Collections.

Union Baptist Church Records, John Parker Research Library, National Underground Railroad Freedom Center, Cincinnati.

University Archives, Mahn Center for Archives and Special Collections, Ohio University Libraries.

## United States Government Documents

DeBow, J. B. D. *Statistical View of the United States Compendium of the Seventh Census: 1854.*

U.S. Federal Population Census, 1830, 1840, 1850, 1860, 1870, 1880, 1890, 1900, 1910.

## Arkansas Government Documents

Arkansas Acts of 1873 (Arkansas State Archives).

Arkansas State Board of Health, Bureau of Vital Statistics: Certificate of Death, Will Corbin.

Jefferson County, Arkansas Probate Record, J. C. Corbin, 1912 Term.

"Report of the Committee to Visit the Branch Normal School." (University of Arkansas Libraries, Fayetteville).

Senate Journal of the State of Arkansas, Twenty-Ninth Session, January 9, 1893.

## Newspapers

*Arkansas Gazette*, September 2, 1875, Little Rock, p. 1, col. 2.

*Chicago Defender*, "Cemetery Ban to Be Hit in Court Suit," November 6, 1962.

*Colored Citizen*, "Colored Public Schools of Cincinnati—Their Faults and Remedies," vol. 29, no. 3, May 19, 1866, p. 2. (Ohio Historical Society).

*Cincinnati Daily Enquirer*, June 23, 1870, p. 4; July 29, 1876.

*East St. Louis Journal*, "Prominent Negro Dies," January 10, 1911, p. 1, col. 5.

*Our Review*, Little Rock and Pine Bluff, Arkansas, May 1915.

*Pine Bluff Graphic*, "Prof. J. C. Corbin Is Found Dead," January 10, 1911.

*Pine Bluff Daily Graphic*, "Inquest Fails to Show Theft Cause," October 8, 1929.

*Pine Bluff Weekly Commercial*, "Prof. J. C. Corbin Is Found Dead," January 12, 1911, p. 8.

*Pine Bluff Commercial*, October 7, 1929, "Well Known Negro Brutally Slain," p. 1.

*The Western Appeal*, January 14, 1911.

## Books

Blassingame, John W. *Black New Orleans, 1860–1880*. Chicago, IL: University of Chicago Press, 1973.

Burns, James J. *Educational History of Ohio*. Columbus, OH: Historical Publishing Co., 1995.

Cromwell, John W. *The Negro in American History: Washington*. The Negro Academy, 1914.

Dabney, W. P. *Cincinnati's Colored Citizens: Historical, Sociological and Biographical*. Cincinnati, OH: Dabney Publishing Co., 1926.

Dillard, Tom, and Roy Reed. *Statesmen, Scoundrels, and Eccentrics: A Gallery of Amazing Arkansans*. Fayetteville: University of Arkansas Press, 2010.

Du Bois, W. E. B. *Black Reconstruction in America*. New York: Athenaeum Press, 1969.

Duncan, Mae Najiyyah. *A Survey of Cincinnati's Black Press & Its Editors 1844-2010*. Xlibris: 2011.

Fisher, Isaac. *Principal's Interrogatory Lecture Course and Other Addresses*. Pine Bluff: University of Arkansas at Pine Bluff, Museum and Cultural Center, 2012.

Foner, Eric. *Freedom's Lawmakers: A Directory of Black Officeholders During Reconstruction*. Oxford University Press, 1993.

Franklin, John Hope. *Reconstruction After the Civil War*. Chicago: University of Chicago Press, 1966.

Gates, Henry Louis, Jr., and Evelyn Brooks Higginbotham, eds. *African American National Biography*, vol. 2. Oxford University Press/Harvard W. E. B. Du Bois Institute, 2008.

Gatewood, Willard B. *Aristocrats of Color: The Black Elite*. Bloomington: Indiana University Press, 1990.

Gerber, David A. *Black Ohio and the Color Line, 1860–1915*. Urbana-Champaign: University of Illinois Press, 1976.

Gordon, Fon Louise. *Caste & Class, The Black Experience in Arkansas, 1880–1920*. Athens: University of Georgia Press, 1995.

Graves, John William. *Town and Country: Race Relations and Urban Development in Arkansas, 1865-1905*. Fayetteville: University of Arkansas Press, 1978.

Hollow, Betty. *Ohio University: The Spirit of a Singular Place, 1804-2004*. Athens: Ohio University Press, 2004.

Huckie, Matt, and Ursula Bielski. *Graveyards of Chicago: The People, History, Art and Lore of Cook County Cemeteries*. Chicago, IL: Lake Claremont Press, 1999.

Leflar, Robert A. *The First 100 Years: Centennial History of the University of Arkansas*. Fayetteville: University of Arkansas Foundation Inc., 1972.

Logan, Rayford W., and Michael Winston. *Dictionary of American Negro Biography*. New York: W. W. Norton, 1982.

Locke, Don C. "Joseph Carter Corbin," in Ohles, J. F. *Biographical Dictionary of American Educators*, 1978.

Moneyhon, Carl H. *Arkansas and the New South 1874–1929*. Fayetteville: University of Arkansas Press, 1997.

Patterson, Thomas E. *History of the Arkansas Teachers Association*. Washington DC: National Education Association, 1981.

Perdreau, Connie. *A Black History of Athens County and Ohio University*. Ohio University, 1988.

Reynolds, John Hugh, and David Yancey Thomas. *History of the University of Arkansas*. Fayetteville: University of Arkansas, 1910.

Simmons, William J. *Men of Mark: Eminent, Progressive and Rising*. Cleveland, OH: Geo M. Rewell & Co., 1887/New York: Arno Press, 1968.

Spear, Allan H. *Black Chicago: The Making of a Negro Ghetto, 1890–1920*. Chicago: University of Chicago Press, 1967.

Washington, Booker T. *An Autobiography: The Story of My Life and Work*. J. L. Nichols & Company, 1901.

———. *Up from Slavery, an Autobiography*. Garden City, NY: Doubleday, Inc., 1901.

## Articles

Arkansas Black History Online. "Biography of Rev. Joseph A. Booker, Little Rock, Arkansas," *Blue Book of Little Rock and Argenta, Arkansas*. Little Rock: Central Printing Co., 1907, 25–26.

Calkins, David. "Black Education and the 19th Century: An Institutional Analysis of Cincinnati Colored Schools." *Cincinnati Historical Society Bulletin* 33 (Fall 1971): 161–171.

Finney, Gladys T. Turner. "Joseph Carter Corbin Educator Extraordinaire." African American Genealogy of the Miami Valley Newsletter, Vol. 8, Issue 2 (April 2009): 6–11.

Gardner, Eric. "Obituary: Joseph Carter Corbin." *The American Mathematical Monthly* (February 1911): 47–48.

"Here and There Among the Alumni." *Ohio Alumnus* (November 1946): 14.

"Joseph Carter Corbin." *Who Was Who in America, 1961–1968.* Vol. 4. Chicago: A. N. Marquis & Company.

Leslie, James W. "Ferd Havis: Jefferson County's Black Republican Leader." *Jefferson County Historical Quarterly* 8, no. 1 (1979): 19–25.

Pearce, Larry Wesley. "American Missionary Association and the Freedmen's Bureau in Arkansas, 1868–1878." *Arkansas Historical Quarterly* 31 (Spring-Winter 1972): 246–261.

Preston, Izola. "Joseph Carter Corbin," in *Arkansas Biography: A Collection of Notable Lives,* ed. Nancy A. Williams. Fayetteville: University of Arkansas Press, 2000.

Preston, Izola, and Marian Morgan. "Joseph Carter Corbin and the Normal School Movement." *Washington County Historical Society Flashback* 42 (February 1992): 22–29.

Rothrock, Thomas. "Joseph Carter Corbin and Negro Education in the University of Arkansas." *Arkansas Historical Quarterly* 30 (Winter 1971): 277–309.

Taylor, David V. "John Quincy Adams: St. Paul Editor and Black Leader." *Minnesota History* 43 (Winter 1973): 283–296.

Wheeler, Elizabeth L. "Isaac Fisher: The Frustrations of a Negro Educator at Branch Normal College, 1902–1911." *Arkansas Historical Quarterly* 41 (Spring 1982): 5–49.

Williams, C. Fred. "Frustration Amidst Hope: The Land Grant Mission of Arkansas AM&N College, 1873–1972." *Agricultural History* 65 (1991): 5–49.

Woodson, Carter G. "The Negroes of Cincinnati Prior to the Civil War." *The Journal of Negro History* 1, no. 1 (January 1916).

## Other Sources

African Americans at Ohio University Timeline, Ohio University Alumni Association.

Amazing African American Leaders of Arkansas, "Joseph Carter Corbin." Educational Poster, Black History Commission of Arkansas.

Biennial Report of the State Superintendent of Public Instruction of the State of Arkansas: Chapter X, "Negro Normals," 1895, 1896 (Arkansas History Commission State Archives).

Chambers, Frederick. "Historical Study of Arkansas Agricultural, Mechanical, and Normal College, 1873–1943." PhD diss., Ball State University, 1970.

Cincinnati City Directory, 1860, 1861, 1868, 1870, 1872, 1873, 1875.

Cook County, Illinois, Death Index, 1878–1922.

Common Schools of Cincinnati 1874–1875 Annual Report and Hand-Book (Cincinnati Public Library).

Graves, John William. "John Gray Lucas." Encyclopedia of Arkansas History & Culture, http://www.encyclopediaofarkansas.net/encyclopedia/entry-detail.aspx?entryID=1700 (accessed January 12, 2017).

*Hamilton County, Ohio Burial Records*, Volume 9, Union Baptist African American Cemetery, Part 1, Hamilton County Chapter of the Ohio Genealogical Society. Compiled and edited by Eleanor Dooks Bardes and Mary H. Remler. Heritage Book, Inc.

Joseph Carter Corbin Will and Probate Court Records (Arkansas State Archives).

"Joseph Carter Corbin, '53," *Ohio University Alumni Bulletin*, April 1909, 26.

John Quincy Adams Obituary, *St. Paul Appeal*, September 9 and 16, 1922.

Little Rock City Directory, 1871, 1872-1873, 1878, 1880, 1881–1882.

Preston, Izola. "Joseph Carter Corbin." Encyclopedia of Arkansas History & Culture, http://www.encyclopediaofarkansas.net/encyclopedia/entry-detail.aspx?entryID=1624 (accessed January 12, 2017).

*The School Visitor*, Volume II, 1881; Volume VI, 1885.

# Index

Freeman, Annie C., 44, 125-128
Freedmen's Aid Society, 33, 131
Fugitive Slave Law of 1850, 20
Futrell, Trustee, 126

Gaines, Eliza, 26
Garland, Gov. Augustus H., 15
Geisreiter, S., 104
German Waldheim Cemetery, 110-112
Grant, President Ulysses S., 35, 135-136
Green, Edward, 112

Harris, William Stephen, 192
Havis, Ferdinand, 106
historically black colleges, 97, 131-132
Holderness Hall, 110
Holland, Milton, 21
Houghton, C. E., 44, 125, 127-128
Howard, Solomon, 21
Hughes, Gov. Simon Pollard, 98

industrial education, 52, 55, 148

Jefferson City, Missouri, 35, 116
Jefferson County display, 50
Jennifer, Alice V., 38
Jim Crow
    Corbin's life during, 56, 116
Johnson, Dr. Calvin, 133
Johnson, N. J. C., 44
Jones, Wiley, 104, 106, 124

Kentucky, 10, 19, 23, 106, 114, 129, 145-147, 151, 153
Kerr, C. V., 121
Knights Templar, 102

land-grant institutions, 43
    See also Morrill Act of 1890.
Langford, William, 108

209

# Additional Support

Publication of this book was made possible in part by an endowment created by Samuel Isaac Bratton (1945–2014), who figured prominently in Arkansas politics and education for more than thirty-five years.

Bratton graduated from Earle High School in Crittenden County, Arkansas, and earned degrees from Hendrix College in Conway and the University of Arkansas School of Law in Fayetteville.

He was a key figure during former president Bill Clinton's time as governor of Arkansas, serving in many posts, including assistant attorney general, liaison for education, and chief counsel for legal and financial policy. He also chaired the Arkansas Public Service Commission. He was known in Arkansas state government for his deft coordination of fiscal and budgetary matters and was instrumental in shepherding many of Governor Clinton's policy initiatives through the state legislature.

Bobby Roberts, former director of the Central Arkansas Library System, said of Bratton: "Sam loved Arkansas and served our citizens for the better part of three decades. His work on education policy and utility regulation issues helped improve all our lives. He was intelligent, hard-working, and fair with everyone. What more could you want or ask from a public servant?"

Printed in the USA
CPSIA information can be obtained
at www.ICGtesting.com
LVHW041320011223
764712LV00001B/13